NATIONAL PLANNING
A S S O C I A T I O N

THE 1992 CHALLENGE
FROM EUROPE:
Development of the
European Community's
Internal Market

Michael Calingaert

The 1992 Challenge from Europe:
Development of the European Community's
Internal Market

NPA Report #237

Price $15.00

ISBN 0-89068-096-5
Library of Congress
Catalog Card Number 88-63005

Printed in the United States of America

 C439

Contents

Chapter 5
How a Single Market Will Change the Community

PART II

Chapter 6
The U.S. Economic Stake in the EC

Chapter 7
Implications of the Integrated Market for U.S. Business

Chapter 8
A Look at Some Sectors

Chapter 9
Implications for U.S. Policy

Preface

The danger exists that Americans, in the private sector as well as in government, do not realize that far-reaching changes are taking place inside the European Community that are at least as significant as the establishment in the 1960s of a customs-free union among the Community's member countries. To the extent the EC's effort is successful in establishing a single, integrated market, it will transform the face of Europe and the way business is conducted in the 12 member states. For that reason, it will be of vital significance to the United States.

That is why I have written this book. It is intended for those who are concerned with U.S. economic interests in the EC, whether they are members of the business community, government officials or other participants in or observers of US-EC relations.

But the subject is vast, and the pace of developments has accelerated. Although it was tempting to seek to cover all aspects of the Community's effort to complete the internal market, such a study not only risked exhaustion of the author and reader but, more important, would have entailed a continual chase after a moving target—at least until the internal market is in fact completed. Accordingly, I have limited the scope of my effort.

My book, then, is selective and impressionistic rather than comprehensive. It is largely based on a distillation of written and oral information I have acquired, plus my own interpretations and assessments. It will not provide a prescription for actions by the private sector; rather, it is intended to raise questions. I hope it will increase the reader's awareness of the changes that are taking place in the EC and of their implications for U.S. interests.

As someone whose life has been intertwined with Europe—through parentage, marriage, academic study, linguistic experience, travel, and diplomatic assignments—it is perhaps not surprising that I should have chosen to turn my attention to what may well be a sea-change in Europe and to attempt to assess what this means for the United States. I trust that in so doing I have made an objective description and appraisal, while bringing an American perspective to this issue.

Acknowledgments

This book could never have been written without the generous assistance of countless individuals and institutions on both sides of the Atlantic. As the study is based largely on information supplied by people, along with their experiences and perceptions, I have depended on the willingness of a wide range of sources to give me their views, answer my questions and help me to wend my way through a very broad subject. Almost without exception, they gave of their time and thoughts extensively and unhesitatingly.

Unfortunately, it is not possible to list all these individuals and institutions; however, I would like to mention at least some of them. To begin with, I want to thank my employer, the Department of State, for giving me a sabbatical year under its Diplomat-in-Residence program and thus providing the opportunity for me to think rather than to act and, more important, to be able to study and write about a major issue of international economic policy without outside guidance or interference.

To my host organization, the National Planning Association, my deep appreciation for providing the institutional backing where, in pleasant surroundings, I could not only pursue my research and writing but also make contacts throughout the U.S. business and trade communities. The support of NPA, including that of many members of NPA committees, contributed immeasurably to the end product. In addition, I gratefully acknowledge the assistance of my research assistant, Sara Krulwich, who saved me much time and effort in tracking down documentation and, particularly, in helping to set out the statistical information in Chapter 6 and Appendixes A–D.

Since I could not have written this study solely on the basis of documentary research and interviews in Washington, I had to undertake a heavy travel schedule, both in the United States and Europe. I am indebted to the German Marshall Fund of the United States which generously provided funds for travel in Europe as well as underwriting the publication and dissemination costs. I am also indebted to Citicorp, E.I. du Pont de Nemours & Co., Inc., Ford Motor Company Fund, McDonald's Corporation, Metropolitan Life Insurance Company, Nabisco Brands Inc., Pfizer International, and Rockwell International for their corporate funding of the project.

On the administrative side, the Delegation of the European Communities in Washington most efficiently provided vital documentation and other information and also organized meetings for me with institutions of the European Community in Brussels. In addition, U.S. diplomatic representatives in Berne, Bonn, Brussels, London, Madrid, Milan, Paris, Rome, and Zurich arranged my visits in Europe, which would have been impossible to set up from Washington.

NPA organized an advisory panel to provide assistance, counsel and critique as I proceeded. I am grateful to the members of the panel, listed below, for generously contributing their time and for helping to focus my thoughts.

EC Internal Market Advisory Panel Members:

PHILIP BRIGGS
Vice Chairman of the Board, Metropolitan Life Insurance Company

CHARLES GOLDMAN
Vice President and Associate General Counsel, ITT Corporation

ARNOLD HANSMANN
Assistant Vice President and International Comptroller, McDonald's Corporation

PAUL J. KOFMEHL
Vice President and Group Executive, IBM World Trade Americas Group

DR. IRENE MEISTER
Vice President, International, American Paper Institute

ANN POLYA
Director, Public Affairs, Pfizer International

RICHARD A. OGREN
Director, International Automotive Operations and Business Strategy, Corporate Strategy Staff, Ford Motor Company

PAUL ROESSEL
Director, Departmental Plans and European Liaison, International Department, E.I. du Pont de Nemours and Company

PETER N. ROGERS
Executive Vice President, International Nabisco Brands

T. DAVID SHEPHERD
Vice President, Europe, Rockwell International Corporation

PHILIP SHERMAN
Senior Vice President, Citicorp

JOAN SPERO
Senior Vice President, International Corporate Affairs, American Express Company

I am particularly indebted to a number of people who offered advice and comments on drafts of my manuscript. This includes the advisory panel, some of whom provided extensive and helpful comments, and numerous government officials who clarified points of fact. In addition, I would like to thank Eammon Bates, Theodore Geiger, Joseph Greenwald, Jacques Pelkmans, Michel Petite, and Daniel Sharp. While I have heeded many of the suggestions I have received, I take full responsibility for this final version.

Finally, I am grateful to my wife Efrem, author of a prize-winning cookbook, who urged me for the past two decades or more to publish and then supported me with unstinting encouragement and understanding as I set about the task at hand.

About the Author

Michael Calingaert is a Foreign Service Officer with long experience in European affairs. A graduate of Swarthmore College, where he majored in European history, he pursued postgraduate studies in history and politics at the University of Cologne under grants from the University and the Fulbright program and in economics at the University of California at Berkeley. During his Foreign Service career, he has specialized in economic affairs in overseas and Washington assignments. His most recent positions have been Minister-Counselor for Economic Affairs at the American Embassies in London and Rome and Deputy Assistant Secretary in the Bureau of Economic and Business Affairs at the Department of State.

Mr. Calingaert undertook his study of "Europe 1992" as Visiting Senior Fellow at the National Planning Association under the Department of State's Diplomat-in-Residence program. However, the views expressed in this book are his own and do not necessarily represent those of the Department.

Executive Summary

The European Community has embarked on an ambitious effort to remove the barriers among the 12 member states to the free movement of goods, services, capital, and people—a process called "completing the internal market" in EC parlance—as was originally envisaged in the establishment of the Common Market. The formal adoption in 1985 of a comprehensive program, which included a timetable for action on specific measures culminating in an overall deadline of December 31, 1992, marked the initiation of a process designed to bring about the most significant change in the European economic landscape in the postwar era.

The decision to proceed was a response to growing concerns that the EC was falling behind its international competitors, particularly the United States and Japan, and that it was paying a heavy cost for the fragmentation of what was to have been a single market. Despite a slow start, momentum was achieved by early 1988 and an irreversible process begun. Key to the momentum were changes in decisionmaking embodied in the Single European Act, resolution of the EC's budgetary impasse and an increasing belief in the EC that the program would succeed. Virtually all member governments have worked actively to increase public awareness of the 1992 program, and EC firms are planning and acting on the assumption that the EC's effort will become a reality.

The program to complete the internal market is contained in a White Paper, which lists about 300 measures or areas requiring action. The barriers targeted for elimination fall into the following categories: border controls; restrictions on the recognition of professional qualifications granted by other member states; differences among member states in value added and excise taxes; differences in legal regimes; restrictions on the free movement of capital; restrictions on the provision of services; differences in regulations and technical standards; and restrictions in public procurement markets. Although the White Paper proposals have been presented as an inseparable package, with no priorities indicated, in fact the key areas are elimination of border controls (the most visible indication of a fragmented market), liberalization of capital movements and services, harmonization of regulations and standards, and the opening of public procurement markets (which account for as much as 15 percent of the EC's gross domestic product).

The effort to complete the internal market takes place within a changing institutional framework. The interplay among the three main EC institutions—the Council, Commission and European Parliament—is characterized by a considerable amount of tension and is affected by the recently expanded powers of the Parliament in the decisionmaking process. Similarly, tension exists between the Brussels institutions (particularly the Commission) and the member states, exacerbated by the gradual shift in responsibility to Brussels. A fourth institution, the European Court of Justice, has taken a number of decisions that have furthered the process of EC economic integration.

While the EC's internal market program has engendered a high level of enthusiasm and support in the Community, the obstacles to success are not insignificant. Most of the issues involved are contentious: countries or groups within them believe they would be adversely affected by particular proposals, and often there are linkages with other issues involving a different set of problems and interests. Despite the strong political consensus in favor of the EC's effort, it will often be difficult to achieve agreement on individual issues. Thus, the path to the single market will not be easy or fast. Indeed, "1992" should be looked upon as a process, not an event. The task will not be completed by 1992, but considerable progress will have been achieved.

More specifically, what are the prospects for action in the various areas by 1992?

- While some diminution in border controls and the costs of cross-border shipment is taking place and will continue, problems relating to different taxes, plant and animal health requirements, and control of drug trafficking, terrorists and immigration will prevent complete elimination of the controls.
- Agreement was recently reached for the mutual recognition among the member states of professional qualifications; however, there is likely to be some resistance and thus results will be somewhat mixed.
- Approximation of indirect taxes will be particularly difficult to achieve because it involves significant changes in the amount and nature of member governments' revenue as well as surrender of control over the sensitive area of taxation policy to Brussels. Slow progress is the most that can be expected.
- Progress on company law is somewhat problematical, in part because of the growing disposition in the EC to address issues of social policy such as working conditions, worker participation and workers rights. On the other hand, action is likely to be completed on the Community trademark, some-

what less likely on the Community patent, and a start made on copyrights. The Commission can be expected to carry out a vigorous competition policy affecting both antitrust issues and state aids.

- The EC has agreed to phase out all remaining restrictions on capital movements by 1992 (and by 1995 at the latest for the weakest member states); however, in view of the threats presented by complete liberalization to the weaker currencies, it is likely that there will be some backsliding.
- Major changes are expected in financial services, primarily through the introduction of a system involving deregulation, harmonization of the essential standards for prudential supervision and protection of investors, mutual recognition among the member states of those standards, and supervision of the institutions by the country in which they are established. Progress is expected to be slower in deregulating transportation and the "new technologies."
- Work under the EC's "new approach" of limiting standards harmonization to "essential requirements" and then providing for mutual recognition of member state standards and the development of European standards by the European bodies is proceeding well, and considerable progress by 1992 is expected. On the other hand, progress on testing and certification is more problematical.
- A major attack is being mounted on the restrictions in public procurement. While a number of significant measures are likely to be in place by 1992, opposition will remain strong and limit effective implementation.

The potential for change in the EC resulting from completion of the internal market is vast. According to an EC-commissioned study, the benefits could be as great as a 7 percent increase in gross domestic product, a 6 percent reduction in prices and the creation of 5 million jobs—all of this presupposing that governments, business and the other economic participants make full use of the opportunities presented. In any event, the process of removing the barriers will create change throughout the Community, and that will affect areas and sectors differently. There will be dislocation and both winners and losers. The net result will be greater competition than before, a situation that will affect all participants in the EC market, whether domestic or foreign.

These developments are of major importance to the United States. The U.S. economic stake in the EC is enormous: the EC accounts for 25 percent of U.S. exports and 40 percent of its foreign investment, and the latter contributes impressively to the EC's economic activity. The creation of a single EC market presents

U.S. business with far-reaching opportunities arising from increased demand, lower costs, increased ease of operation, and potential economies of scale. At the same time, it must be recognized that these opportunities will similarly be available to EC and third country firms.

The key question for U.S. business interests is whether, and if so to what extent, completion of the internal market will be accompanied by measures that limit opportunities for U.S. firms. The areas where U.S. interests will be vitally affected are regulation of services, regulations and standards, and public procurement. Although there is clearly no basic predisposition by the EC to establish a "Fortress Europe" to the exclusion of outsiders, pressures exist in the EC both for and against a measure of protection or at least extracting concessions from other countries in return for the benefits their firms will derive from the single market. The outcome of that debate will be affected not only by a balancing of interests within the EC, but also by the economic climate, the state of US-EC relations, and the extent to which the EC considers it necessary to protect itself against perceived unequal treatment by the Japanese.

The specific areas where U.S. export interests could be adversely affected are the extension of national import restrictions to an EC-wide basis on products manufactured in the United States (e.g., Japanese automobiles) and restrictive antidumping measures. For U.S. investors the areas are limitations in the application of the principle of national treatment, institution of a requirement that reciprocal treatment be granted EC firms in the United States in certain sectors (e.g., financial services), restrictive interpretation of rules of origin, and the introduction of unduly restrictive social legislation. Finally, both exporters and investors would be disadvantaged by a nontransparent standards-setting process resulting in European standards that do not conform with or lead to global standards and a public procurement regime that limits U.S. participation.

U.S. firms presently or potentially doing business in the EC ignore these developments at their own peril. What should they do? They should gather information through the variety of sources available, review and develop their strategies to take account of the evolving situation, and seek to influence the decisionmaking process in the EC.

It is essential that the U.S. government closely monitor developments in the EC and seek to avoid actions by the EC that would adversely affect U.S. interests. Particular attention should be paid to import quotas, national treatment, reciprocity, and the effect of the EC's movement toward a single market on early and successful conclusion of the Uruguay Round of trade negotiations.

While many Americans believe that the United States is often not privy to EC internal deliberations at an early enough stage to influence the outcome on issues where important U.S. interests are involved, that situation may be improved by the increasing openness of the EC institutions.

An irreversible process is under way, offering the promise of a fundamental transformation of the EC. Opportunities await participants in that market, and U.S. firms should expect to be able to operate in the EC on equal terms with their competitors. Nonetheless, problems are bound to arise, and the government will need to seek to ensure equal treatment for U.S. firms in a highly competitive market.

Introduction

America's economic gaze has increasingly shifted in recent years from Europe to the Pacific. This is hardly surprising. The world has evolved from the economic bipolarity of the United States and Europe in the early postwar period to an ever more complex web of economic interrelationships involving all areas. U.S. relations—and problems—with Japan and other Asian countries have increased. With the fastest economic growth in the world taking place in that area, U.S. trade with Asia has overtaken that with Europe. Meanwhile, the enthusiasm in the United States generated by the Treaty of Rome in 1957, which, in a step of vast economic and political implications, established the European Economic Community,* has been replaced by a quieter relationship between two roughly equal partners. And in more recent years, the Community has endured a period of indifferent development, characterized by economic rigidities, decreasing competitiveness and anemic growth, encapsuled in the term "Euro-sclerosis."

But while the attention of U.S. economic interests has been directed more to the Pacific than to the Atlantic, the European Community has embarked on an extensive, ambitious program to remove the myriad of barriers impeding the free movement of goods, services, people, and capital among the member states to create in fact what has existed more in name—a real Common Market. This effort to establish a single, integrated market is called, in EC parlance, "completing the internal market." The program is formalized in a White Paper, issued in 1985, that lists 300 measures the Community must adopt to reach its goal by the end of 1992. By 1988, the issues grouped under the "internal market" heading had formed the centerpiece of the Community's agenda; they now represent the main subject of debate and action among the EC's 12 member states.

---

* The European Economic Community entered into existence on January 1, 1958. At that time it joined two other Communities—Coal and Steel, and Atomic Energy—to form the European Communities, which became the official name. However, it is now common practice to refer simply to the European Community as encompassing any or all of the Communities, and that term is used here. The 12 member states comprising the EC are Belgium, Denmark, France, Germany, Greece, Ireland, Italy, Luxembourg, the Netherlands, Portugal, Spain, and the United Kingdom.

In essence, the book covers two issues regarding the EC's program to complete the internal market: what is happening in the EC and what that means for U.S. interests. Certain issues have consciously been avoided, or at least touched on only lightly, because they did not appear central to the completion of the internal market or to U.S. interests, or because of limitations of time and space. These include agricultural policy, energy issues, defense industry concerns, and the European research and development (R&D) programs. Wherever possible, information is current through the middle of 1988.

Part I begins the analysis of the EC's efforts on "Europe 1992" by describing, in Chapter 1, the absence of a single, integrated market and the launching of the internal market program. Chapter 2 describes the institutional framework under which the program is being carried out. In Chapter 3, the barriers that the program is designed to overcome are enumerated. Chapter 4 looks ahead to the scheduled completion date of 1992, reviewing the various factors that will affect the extent of the program's success, and then examines the actions intended, taking place and likely to take place in removing the various barriers. Chapter 5 considers the consequences for the Community of the internal market program, based on studies and recent developments, including some political implications.

Part II turns to the implications for U.S. interests, beginning with a brief description in Chapter 6 of the economic importance to the United States of its exports to and investment in the Community. Present and potential EC attitudes toward non-EC firms are examined in Chapter 7, which also reviews opportunities and risks for U.S. exporters and investors and provides some thoughts on how U.S. business can best prepare for "1992." Chapter 8 consists of brief descriptions of issues affecting U.S. firms in six selected manufacturing and service sectors. Consideration is given in Chapter 9 to issues the U.S. government will have to face with the evolution of the EC into an integrated market and the appropriate role for public policy. Conclusions are presented in Chapter 10.

— PART I —

Toward the Goal of a Single Market

The establishment of the European Economic Community in 1957 was an event of epochal importance. While the EC is taken for granted today as a part of the political and economic landscape, its formation represented a revolutionary departure from hundreds of years of history. In place of fully sovereign, independent countries, each carrying out its own economic policies, the founding members agreed to give up some of their sovereignty and independence by merging a considerable part of their separate economic systems into a single unit. Accordingly, Europe—at least the major countries—would be able to grow and prosper in a way that would not have been possible had the countries elected to continue down separate paths.

The intention of the Community's founders was that the Common Market, as it has popularly been called since its inception, would be just that. This was made clear in the Preamble and Articles 2 and 3 of the Treaty of Rome, which established the European Economic Community. Although the Preamble is couched in general terms, it resolves to "eliminate the barriers which divide Europe," calls for the removal of existing obstacles and asserts the need to strengthen the "unity" of the member states' economies.

Article 2 is more specific, listing a number of objectives as the "task" of the Community. These are to be accomplished by "establishing a common market and progressively approximating the economic policies of the member states." Article 3 then sets out the "activities" the Community will undertake to achieve these objectives. The first is the elimination of duties and quantitative restrictions among the member states as well as measures having equivalent effect. The Article goes on to call for the establishment of a common customs tariff and a common commercial policy toward third countries, the abolition of obstacles to the free movement of people, services and capital, and a number of other common policies.

None of these steps toward formation of a Common Market was expected to be accomplished overnight. The first, vital step was the progressive removal of tariffs among the member states, which were to be abolished over 12 years. That this was accomplished 18 months ahead of schedule, in mid-1968, was an indication of the momentum and enthusiasm of the early years. It also reflected a favorable economic climate, in which general prosperity—in part the result of the trade generated among the member states—made it easier to move forward with trade liberalization.

Removal of internal tariff barriers was a very significant step—economically in that it facilitated and expanded trade between member countries and psychologically in that it promoted the idea and practice of conducting economic activity across member country borders. During its first three decades, the EC made considerable progress toward the goal of a Common Market: not only tariffs but also quotas were abolished between member countries; a common structure was established for indirect taxation; most restrictions were removed on the use of foreign exchange for trade transactions and capital investment; EC external trade policy was placed in Community hands; judicial decisions limited the ability of member states to maintain regulations restricting the importation of products from other EC countries; and a start was made in product standardization. At the same time, however, vast areas of economic activity remained untouched either because they were not addressed or because of an impasse among the member states.

THE UNCOMMON MARKET

In addition to the inherent difficulty of reducing or removing barriers—particularly under a system that required unanimous consent for most important decisions—the situation was exacerbated by the economic climate of the 1970s. The oil shocks of 1973–74 and 1978–79, the inflationary pressures of the mid-1970s and the widespread recession brought about political and economic forces that combined to protect what were deemed to be national interests at the expense of promoting Community-wide policies. Further impeding progress were the administrative and financial burdens caused by the accession of three new members to the EC in 1973 and one more in 1981. As a result, instances increased in which member states raised barriers against other members, though usually not overtly. Progress toward a real Common Market slowed to a snail's pace; maintenance of the status quo was the most that could be hoped for.

Evidence of the "uncommon market" abounded and was the cause of mounting frustration within the Community. Examples were sobering, if not ludicrous.

- As members of the European Community Youth Orchestra traveled within the Community, they had to carry documentary evidence of their instruments' country of origin and often had to deposit the value of their instruments when leaving their home country to satisfy customs authorities that they had not exported the instruments.

- Because of delays at the borders between member countries, a 750-mile trip from London to Milan took 58 hours (excluding the Channel crossing), whereas a trip of equal length within the United Kingdom took only 36 hours.[1]
- A consumer organization estimated that a person traveling through 10 member countries (excluding Ireland and Luxembourg) and returning to the starting country would end up with only 53 percent of the money with which he or she began because of the cost of changing money into local currency.[2]
- A European television manufacturer had to make seven types of television sets to meet member country standards, which required 70 engineers to adjust new models to individual country requirements and cost an additional $20 million per year.[3]
- EC members argued for 10 years, including at the ministerial level, over setting standards for fork-lift trucks before coming to a decision—the main point of contention being the most appropriate pedal system.
- The cost of automobile insurance varied by about 300 percent among EC member countries and the cost of telephone service by 50 percent.[4]

By the early 1980s, the forces for change were beginning to be felt both inside the EC institutions and in the private sector. Impelling these forces was a combination of three interrelated concerns:

- economic stagnation characterized by indifferent growth, high unemployment and increasingly recognized structural rigidities, all falling under the rubric of "Euro-sclerosis";
- increased competition confronting enterprises in the Community from the outside—the United States and particularly Japan and the other Asian nations—especially in high technology areas; and
- the seeming inability of the Community to function as an institution and to resolve problems, ranging from the British contribution to the EC budget to agricultural policy.

The EC's executive arm, the Commission (discussed in Chapter 2), sought to raise the level of awareness in the Community about the lack of progress in establishing a truly integrated market and the consequences thereof. In 1981, it issued a communication on the state of the internal market, followed the next year by one listing sectors of priority importance that it considered ripe for decision. Another communication, also in 1982, described a number of obstacles to free movement across intra-Community borders and asked "how . . . can citizens and business circles, who have to live from day to day with this state of affairs, be expected to believe that the Community exists?"[5] Going beyond the rhetoric, the Commission set forth concrete proposals for action.

Pressures also rose for action in the European Parliament. At Parliament's request, a French civil servant and a British academic drew up a report on the EC's economic crisis and on the ways and means of bringing about an economic recovery. The resulting Albert-Ball report, issued in 1983, concluded that "the European market is still far from common: it is a kind of economic equivalent of feudalism."[6] The report went on to calculate some of the costs of "non-Europe," such as a waste of $48 billion from restrictive public procurement practices and $14 billion from delays to truck transportation at the internal borders (these costs equaled about 2 percent of the Community's GDP).[7] The report concluded that solutions had to be sought in a Community-wide context.

At the same time, voices were increasingly raised in the EC business community. Most prominent was the president of the Dutch electronics firm Philips, who sounded the alarm that the EC's inability to move toward completion of the internal market—or, as he put it, its failure to complete the homework given in the Treaty of Rome—was the cause of the Community's deteriorating competitive position. Citing the need for urgent action—and calling for "Europessimism" to make way for "Eurorealism"—he drew up a plan of measures to be taken over a five-year period, using the slogan "Europe 1990."[8]

As the concerns and pressures rose, the Community finally moved to address the issue of its internal market in a comprehensive and systematic fashion.

THE PROGRAM IS LAUNCHED

The process by which the EC initiated its formal program to complete the internal market was a series of undertakings and decisions of the European Council, the semiannual meeting of the heads of government of the member states. At its meeting in Copenhagen in December 1982, the representatives pledged action on pending priority measures to "reinforce" the internal market. In Fontainebleau in mid-1984, the Council called for a study of measures to abolish border controls between member countries. At the Dublin meeting at the end of the year, the Council agreed that steps should be taken to complete the internal market. Finally, in Brussels in March 1985, the Council endorsed the goal of a single market by 1992 and called upon the Community's executive agency—the European Commission—to draw up a detailed program with a specific timetable.

Key factors in launching the program were the Commission's new president, Jacques Delors, and new commissioner responsible for the internal market, Lord Cockfield, who took office as part of the quadrennial changeover at the beginning of 1985. Delors, a former Finance Minister in the French government, was eager to inject a new dynamism into the Community. As he reviewed areas for possible major initiatives, he concluded that the only feasible one was the effort to complete the internal market. With the backing of the Council, Delors got the project off the ground.

The White Paper

Drawing on considerable work already undertaken, the Commission issued a White Paper entitled "Completing the Internal Market" in June 1985.[9] This document enumerates the measures that need to be taken, or the areas to be addressed, for the Community to achieve that goal. At its meeting in Milan the same month, the European Council endorsed the White Paper's objective and pledged the Community to completion of the internal market by the end of 1992. That date was selected to coincide with the end of the next Commission's term of office, thus providing for completion within the period of two Commissions. Lord Cockfield, a former government official, businessman and cabinet member in the United Kingdom, was responsible for the drafting of the White Paper. He has pushed implementation of the program with dedication and determination and thus can take much of the credit for the substantial progress already achieved.

The White Paper divides the obstacles to an integrated market into three categories of barriers—physical, technical and fiscal (see Appendix E). In addition to explaining the philosophical underpinning of its proposals (largely written by Lord Cockfield),[10] the White Paper describes the nature of the impediments and the kinds of actions that will be necessary under each category. In an annex to the report, the Commission lists approximately 300 specific areas for action—including reference to its numerous previous proposals—and sets dates for submission of its proposals, action by the Council and ultimate entry into effect. All dates fall within the agreed-upon deadline of December 31, 1992.

As it launched the Community on the road to an integrated internal market, the White Paper made clear the importance it attached to the occasion: "Europe stands at the cross-roads. Either we go ahead—with resolution and determination—or we drop back into mediocrity. . . . The time for talk has now passed. The time for action has come. That is what the White Paper is about."[11]

But what remained ambiguous—and probably unavoidably so—is the definition of the "completed internal market" or "single, integrated market" that the Community set out to achieve. Even though the White Paper, as the sole official document, defines the integrated market in a formal sense, there is no standard against which to measure the proposed and actual Community actions. One is left with the general notion of a market with "no differential of economic significance attached to national frontiers or the residence and nationality of the economic agents of the member states."[12]

In its introduction, the White Paper makes clear that it does not purport to cover every possible issue affecting the integration of the member states' economies. Rather, it focuses on measures it deems "directly necessary to achieve a single, integrated market" inside the Community.[13] As the Paper states, other measures and issues will affect the process. Some of these were consciously omitted, while others have assumed greater or lesser importance as circumstances have changed. Thus, some modifications to the White Paper have been made over time. For instance, in 1988 the Commission eliminated some issues no longer deemed sufficiently important, thereby reducing its list of measures to 285.

Although it is appropriate to focus on the White Paper, an analysis of the EC's program to complete the internal market must look beyond the specific provisions of the White Paper because the key question is the extent to which the Community succeeds in eliminating the fragmentation of the market. Action, or inaction, by EC institutions will occur in a number of fields not specifically covered in the White Paper that will be directly relevant to the success of the Community's effort; further, actions by national governments (and to a lesser extent other public authorities) as well as private companies and individuals are necessary to make the single market a reality. Indeed, their role will be crucial, in steps ranging from rapid and effective implementation of Community policies by member governments to company decisions on corporate organization and operation.

The Single European Act

As the Community began to look seriously at integration, it recognized that a major impediment to progress was the broad applicability of unanimity in Council voting, as set forth in the Treaty of Rome, and the vitiation of majority voting through the so-called Luxembourg Compromise of 1966, under which any member state could block a vote in the Council by invoking a "vital national interest." Consequently, a consensus developed to institute a decisionmaking procedure involving widespread use of something less than unanimity that would meet the political imperatives of the member states. At their Milan session in mid-1985, the EC heads of government agreed to a negotiating conference to amend the Treaty for this and other purposes. The negotiations were conducted with dispatch, resulting in passage of the Single European Act, which was signed at the end of 1985 and entered into force in mid-1987.

The Single European Act—the only major constitutional change in the EC—was the final, critical element in the launch of the program to complete the internal market. The act improved the voting procedure significantly by extending the use of weighted voting, a so-called qualified majority, to all issues relating to the internal market except taxation (a rather considerable exception), professional qualifications and the rights and interests of employees. Under this system, votes are apportioned among the member countries in accordance with their size, with the four largest members (France, Germany, Italy, and the United Kingdom) receiving the maximum number of votes. No single member state can constitute a blocking minority, as in the past; rather, two large and one small member or one large and three small members or various combinations of small members are required. Although these amendments to the voting procedures do not go as far as some would have liked—one critic referred to the act as "a loophole dressed up as a Treaty" insofar as the internal market is concerned[14]—they assuredly facilitate the decisionmaking process. Instead of the veto power held by each, member states must work out political compromises through coalition building and horse trading. As a result, certain member states can work more closely together to promote regional or other shared interests—for example, the Mediterranean countries.

The Single European Act goes well beyond provisions for Council voting. It includes a member state commitment to complete the internal market by expressing the Community's "firm political will" to take the necessary decisions, in particular the measures set out in the White Paper, before January 1, 1993. Certain other provisions of the Single European Act will affect activity on the internal market, most directly the enhanced power of the European Parliament (see Chapter 2). In addition, the act commits the EC to the objectives of increased "economic and social cohesion" (a code phrase for seeking to diminish the unevenness of economic development among the EC's different regions), a common scientific and technological development policy, further development of the European Monetary System (EMS), and coordinated action on the environment. All of these could directly impinge on the program to complete the internal market.

NOTES

1. Paolo Cecchini, *The European Challenge 1992* (Wildwood House, Aldershot [U.K.], 1988), p. 12.
2. "Oh for a monnet," *The Economist,* July 16, 1988, p. 44.
3. Speech by EC Commission official Mathew Cocks, American Chamber of Commerce (U.K.), London, June 16, 1988.
4. Cecchini, *European Challenge,* p. 4.
5. "Strengthening the Internal Market," Commission document, COM(82) 399, June 24, 1982, p. 1.
6. Michel Albert and James Ball, *Toward European Economic Recovery in the 1980s: Report to the European Parliament* (New York: Praeger Special Studies, 1984).
7. The dollar figures are conversions of European Currency Unit. For simplicity and uniformity, these have been calculated throughout the study at ECU 1.00 = U.S. $1.20, which was the approximate exchange rate as of mid-1988. For an explanation of the ECU, see footnote 5, Chapter 3.
8. Proposals are contained in "Europe 1990," speech by Dr. W. Dekker, Centre for European Policy Studies, Brussels, November 13, 1984; reference to "Europessimism" and "Eurorealism" in "Europe 1990: an Agenda for Action," speech by Dr. W. Dekker, Deutsche Gesellschaft fur Auswaertige Politik E.V., Bonn, October 9, 1985.
9. "Completing the Internal Market" (White Paper from the Commission to the European Council, Milan, June 28–29, 1985), COM(85) 310, June 14, 1985. This was also issued as a separate publication by the Office for Official Publications of the European Communities, Luxembourg, 1985.
10. "The Completion of the Internal Market," speech by Lord Cockfield, Institute for International Economics, Washington, May 24, 1988.
11. COM(85) 310, paragraph 219, and quoted in "First Report from the Commission to the Council and the European Parliament on the implementation of the Commission's White Paper on completing the internal market," COM(86) 300, May 26, 1986, p. 23.
12. Jacques Pelkmans and Alan Winters, *Europe's Domestic Market,* Royal Institute of International Affairs Chatham House Papers No. 43 (London: Routledge, 1988), p. 4.
13. COM(85) 310, paragraph 17.
14. "The Politics of the Internal Market," speech by member of the European Parliament Gijs de Vries, British Chamber of Commerce for Belgium and Luxembourg, Brussels, March 24, 1987.

The EC's Institutional Framework | 2

Before proceeding with a discussion of the barriers that impede the establishment of a single market, it is necessary to describe the institutional framework within which decisions are taken in the Community, in particular the roles of the various institutions and the interaction among them. The primary EC institutions are the Council, the Commission, the Parliament, and the European Court of Justice.[1] The Council and the Commission are headquartered in Brussels; although the Parliament and Court are situated in Luxembourg, Brussels is generally considered the capital of the Community.

THE MAIN INSTITUTIONS

The *Council* is the supreme decisionmaking body, which consists of representatives of the 12 member states. Decisions are taken either by unanimity (with each state exercising an equal vote) or by qualified majority voting (see Chapter 1), depending on the issue. The Council meets two or three times a year at the head-of-government level, known as the European Council, where it seeks to set general policy and resolve deadlocked issues. However, most of the important work is carried out among member country ministers with the same portfolio in periodic meetings. Thus, for example, the Agriculture Ministers meet as the Agricultural Council, the Finance Ministers as the Economic and Finance Council and so on. Chairmanship of the Council—or Councils— rotates by six-month periods among the member states, following the alphabetical order of names of the countries in their own language. During that period, the country in question holds the presidency of the Council, and as such it represents or speaks on behalf of the EC internationally on most issues.

Since issuance of the White Paper, the Council has made two procedural innovations with a view to increasing the effectiveness of its work on the internal market. First, it established an Internal Market Council, consisting of ministers from different ministries involved in decisions arising from the White Paper, even though these might otherwise have been dealt with in a different council. For example, the Council would consider and take decisions on wide-ranging topics such as financial services, merger policy, public procurement, and technical standards. Second, it was decided to establish a "rolling work program" in 1985, whereby the three member governments holding the previous, present and next Council presidency would coordinate the subjects and measures on which decisions would be sought during the six-month presidency, rather than leaving it solely to the preferences of the incumbent member country.

As the executive arm of the EC, the *Commission* drafts proposals for Council decision—the only body that can do so—and as such is the initiator of Community policy. It performs numerous other functions, from administering EC expenditures to rule making and carrying out common Community policies, based on authority granted by the Council and certain Treaty provisions. Consisting of a bureaucracy of about 12,000 EC civil servants, the Commission is headed by a group of 17 commissioners (one or two from each country, depending on its size), selected by the national governments for a four-year term. Although there is no coordination or consultation among member governments regarding their selection of commissioners, the Commission's president is elected by the European Council from among national government nominees or, in fact, on the basis of a consensus. It then falls to the president to apportion the specific responsibilities of the commissioners based on political considerations and qualifications.

Playing a somewhat ambiguous role, the *European Parliament* is the only democratically established body, consisting since 1979 of representatives directly elected by EC citizens. Elections for Parliament's 518 seats are held every five years (at the same time in all countries) on the basis of individual electoral systems determined by each member state. The members of Parliament do not sit or act as national blocs, but rather are organized into eight cross-country political groupings, covering the spectrum from left to right.

Particularly prior to the Single European Act, the power of Parliament was circumscribed. Apart from its thus far unused power to dismiss the 17 commissioners and its limited consultative role in pending legislation, the Parliament had the last word on noncompulsory EC expenditure (i.e., the 30 percent or so not required by Community legislation) and had, and used, the authority to reject the EC's annual budget. Beyond this it could only advise—and delay. Not surprisingly, Parliament's weakness vis-a-vis the other two institutions was a source of frustration to its members as was its limited influence despite being the body most directly representing the citizens of the Community.

However, the Single European Act, which entered into force in mid-1987, significantly enhanced the role of Parliament. By a majority vote of its total membership, Parliament can now reject applications for membership in the EC as well as trade and other agreements negotiated with non-EC countries. But most important, the act strengthened the position of Parliament in the Community's legislative process.

The *European Court of Justice* consists of 13 judges (at least one per member state) named to six-year terms by the mutual consent of the member states. The Court has responsibilities rather similar to those of the U.S. Supreme Court, although it is far less publicly visible. The Court interprets the Treaty of Rome, rules on the conformity of member state actions with the Treaty and with EC legislation, and resolves disputes involving the other Community institutions, including ones relating to their actions and competence. Cases can be brought by national governments, persons (operating through the relevant national court system) and the EC institutions, and the national courts must ask the Court for guidance when issues of EC law are involved.

THE DECISIONMAKING PROCESS

Formal decisions by the EC institutions take one of four forms. Most important are directives, which are drafted by the Commission, considered by the Parliament and then adopted by the Council (see below). Once that has happened, the directives become binding on the member states, which are responsible for transposing them into national laws or regulations. Regulations, which follow the same general approval procedure, are usually more limited in scope, such as spelling out details of a decision already taken. They become effective and have the force of law upon adoption by the Council. Together, directives and regulations constitute the Community's body of law. Finally, there are non-binding recommendations, which encourage member states to act in a certain way, and "decisions," which are generally executive actions, such as formal adoption of international agreements.

The procedures for adopting directives and regulations were changed by the Single European Act. Parliament now has two formal opportunities to consider Commission proposals under what is known as the "cooperation procedure." At the first reading, when the Commission sends proposed directives and regulations to the Council, Parliament can submit its opinion. The Commission and Council must take this into account in revising the proposal for a second reading. Amendments passed at that time by a two-thirds majority of Parliament's membership, if accepted by the Commission, will be adopted unless overturned by a unanimous vote of the Council. Thus, if Parliament does achieve a fairly large degree of consensus, as it has on occasion (for example, on budgetary issues), it can wield extensive power.

The interplay among the three institutions is, of course, dynamic and has been characterized by a considerable amount of tension on all sides. Over time, the Commission has amassed substantial power, if for no reason other than that the Council is unable to keep up with the complexities of all issues and of necessity must delegate authority, or otherwise see it flow, to the Commission. Consequently, there has been some concern in the Council that the Commission was moving beyond its delegated authority or competence—in a sense becoming too much of a power on its own. At the same time, the Commission has criticized the Council for being too slow-moving and ineffective in taking decisions,[2] in its view reflecting the member governments' inability or unwillingness to subordinate national interests to the good of the Community. For its part, Parliament has felt the frustrations of impotence, exacerbated by the resistance of the two other bodies to sharing power with it.

The new element in this three-way relationship is the expanded role in the decisionmaking process accorded Parliament by the Single European Act. Since the act has been in force only since July 1987, it is premature to gauge how Parliament will use its newly acquired power. At a minimum, a significant change in attitude and mode of operation will be necessary to enable it to take advantage of the opportunities presented by the act—and that will not be easy after so many years in a subordinate role. However, Parliament clearly wants to increase its relevance and influence, and over time that is likely to happen.

In any event, increased interaction can be expected among the three institutions, with greater attention being paid by the Commission and Council to Parliament, as a semblance of a triangular "checks and balances" system develops. Both Parliament and the Commission may desire, or be able, to play the other two institutions off against each other; more likely, however, they will find a greater convergence of interests, as both represent "European interests" desirous of promoting the Community as an institution and EC-wide solutions to issues, whereas the Council is by its nature more protective of and responsive to national interests. Nonetheless, the Commission will find Parliament "intrusive" and "difficult" in some areas previously not its preserve, and that could exacerbate relations.

Although not a direct participant in the decisionmaking process, the European Court of Justice has played an important, dynamic role in the development of the Community and particularly in its economic integration. A serious problem now facing the Court is its rapidly growing case load. While the judicial process is relatively slow under the best of circumstances, the average time for a Court decision is now about 18 months, and 527 cases were pending at the end of 1987 compared with 395 a year earlier and 135 in 1975.³ To mitigate this problem, the Council approved the establishment in mid-1988 of a Court of First Instance, as envisaged by the Single European Act; this court will handle simpler competition cases as well as EC staff matters. While this should lessen the burden, it will take some time for the lower court to enter into operation. In any event, litigation before the Court is expected to increase as a result of pressures created by the internal market program, for example in connection with competition policy and the interpretation of the Single European Act's provision enabling member states in certain circumstances to adopt more stringent standards than those agreed to under qualified majority voting in the Council.

Although some observers believe the Court has played too passive a role, declining to go beyond the specific issues presented to it,⁴ it has rendered many significant decisions on internal market issues and can reasonably be expected to continue to do so. Most notable have been:

- In the landmark Cassis de Dijon decision of 1979, the Court upheld the Commission's refusal to allow Germany to keep out a French alcoholic beverage because it did not satisfy German standards (insufficient alcoholic content), since the product was legally produced in France. In this case, and subsequent interpretations, the Court accepted the principle that a product legally produced and marketed in one member state must have the right to move freely throughout the Community unless an importing member country could demonstrate that its exclusion was based on genuine issues of public health and safety.⁵

- Along similar lines but on issues of greater prominence and interest, in 1987 the Court outlawed Germany's 16th century so-called purity laws, which restricted sales of beer in Germany to products containing specified ingredients, and in 1988 ruled against an Italian prohibition on the sale of pasta products not made exclusively from durum (hard) wheat. In the latter case, the Court ruled that importation of German pasta, which was made from mixed hard and soft wheat, was neither prejudicial to the consumer's health nor misleading. It also rejected as irrelevant the Italian argument that decreased use of durum would run counter to the EC's agricultural policies and add to the Community's budgetary expenditures.

- In the 1986 Nouvelles Frontieres decision, involving a complaint by a French travel agency against French restrictions, the Court for the first time confirmed the applicability of EC competition rules to civil aviation.
- Finally, in a series of four decisions on insurance at the end of 1986, the Court, though with some ambiguity, moved toward the principle that a company legally established in one member country could write policies in another without having to establish a branch or subsidiary there.

COMPETITION POLICY

A final, crucial element of the process involved in completion of the internal market is competition policy. While this is obviously not an institutional issue, it is included in this chapter because it involves an activity of the Commission.

Although clearly recognized as an integral element in forming an integrated EC market, competition policy was not included in the White Paper because it is covered in the Treaty of Rome,[6] in fact, it is one of the few areas in which the Treaty gives power directly to the Commission. In recent years, the Commission has played a much more activist role than previously. As the responsible commissioner has pointed out, the Commission is the sole authority, serving as investigator, prosecutor, judge, and jury (although its decision can be appealed to the European Court of Justice).[7]

The two areas of most intense Commission activity have been mergers and other forms of concentration among enterprises, and government subsidies and other assistance to regions and economic sectors (known as "state aids"). In the Commission's view, competition policy will play a key role in ensuring that the market opening that results from completion of the internal market yields the expected benefits and is not replaced by divisions of markets stemming from restrictive business practices or member state protectionist measures. Thus, it is the task of competition policy to control actions by government and by enterprises.[8]

Commission involvement is bound to increase in both areas. On the one hand, there has been a sharp increase in mergers, acquisitions and other business combinations across country borders, partly as a result of the prospective creation of a single market. On the other hand, as competition increases and economic dislocation takes place, governments will be under increasing pressure to provide or augment assistance to affected regions, industrial sectors, enterprises, and/or workers.

NOTES

1. For a fuller description of the EC institutions, see Emile Noel, former Secretary-General of the Commission, *The Institutions of the European Community* (Office for Official Publications of the European Communities, Luxembourg, 1985).

2. For example, in "Second Report from the Commission to the Council and the European Parliament on the implementation of the Commission's White Paper on completing the internal market," COM(87) 203, May 11, 1987, p. 7, the characterizations of the Council's performance on the internal market program in 1986 were: "a most disappointing result," "failure of the Council . . . to instill a new and necessary sense of urgency."

3. "Commission supports junior branch of European Court to ease case burden," *Financial Times*, May 6, 1988.

4. See, for example, "Freedom of movement for services in the European Community," European Service Industries Forum, Keerbergen, February 1988.

5. The decisions were based on Articles 30–36 of the Treaty. These articles, crucial to completion of the internal market, deal with the prohibition of quantitative restrictions on trade among the member countries and measures having equivalent effect. For a discussion of the legal issues, see Laurence W. Gormley, *Prohibiting Restrictions on Trade within the EEC* (Amsterdam: Elsevier Science Publishers, 1985).

6. Treaty of Rome Article 85 covers restrictive business practices; Article 86, abuses of dominant position; Article 90, member state-controlled enterprises; and Articles 92–94, state aids.

7. "European Unity and EEC Competition Law," speech by Commissioner Peter D. Sutherland, St. Louis Bar Association, St. Louis, May 10, 1985.

8. "16th Report on Competition Policy" (Brussels: Commission of the European Communities, 1987).

What Are the Barriers $\quad$ 3

Despite the numerous political and economic changes that have taken place in the Community over the past 30 years—and many of these have been fundamental—the EC remains to a considerable extent a grouping of individual countries with separate economic systems. The barriers that impede the free movement of people, goods, services, and capital among the member states can be divided into three categories: those representing basic historical and cultural differences; those not covered by the White Paper; and those that are the object of the measures included in the White Paper.

The first category consists of the very significant differences that reflect hundreds of years of historical development. Physical and cultural differences among the member countries are quite obvious. Differences in language, tradition and ways of thinking and acting in many respects impede the establishment of a single market, and although their effect is difficult to identify and quantify, their importance should not be underestimated. While these differences (and their significance) among EC member countries will continue to diminish, this is a very long-term process and is affected only marginally and indirectly by actions of governments and the Community (but more so by modern telecommunications and other nongovernmental factors).

The second category of barriers consists of economic factors that directly affect the operation of the market but are not included in the White Paper. Notable among these are:

- Absence of a common currency. While the EC has benefited from the considerable success of the European Monetary System in reducing the fluctuations among, and in some cases instability of, the currencies of member countries, the U.K.'s refusal to join the exchange rate mechanism of the EMS and, more particularly, the absence of a common currency in the member states increases the complexity and cost of doing business in the EC.
- Lack of coordination of macroeconomic policies. The pursuit by member governments of different macroeconomic objectives and policies, especially monetary, with no fully developed

mechanism or requirement for coordination, creates obstacles to the liberalization of capital movements.
- Differences in direct taxation regimes. Although the White Paper addresses some differences in indirect taxes, it makes no reference to direct personal taxation; further, corporate taxation systems, which are characterized by disparate structures and rates—with implications for competition and decisions on investment—are covered only regarding "cooperation" between firms in different member states.
- Differences in social, environmental and consumer policies (only indirectly dealt with in the White Paper). Generally reflecting diverse philosophies and historical circumstances of the member countries, these differences have resulted in a lack of uniform treatment in regulations and laws, which inevitably affects competition and decisions on investment.

Two areas that bear directly on the EC's effort to complete the internal market, although not included in the White Paper, are nonetheless the subject of parallel action. One is telecommunications, on which the Commission has initiated work on deregulation and liberalization with a view to forming an EC-wide market for equipment and services by the end of 1992. The other is competition policy, an area in which the Commission was already active under authority granted by the Treaty of Rome. These subjects are treated in detail in Chapters 8 and in 2 and 4, respectively.

The third category, then, consists of barriers addressed by the White Paper. Rather than following the somewhat awkward subdivisions of the White Paper, an eight-heading breakdown is used here.

(1) Border Controls

The physical, visible controls on individuals and goods at the borders between member states are the most obvious, tangible evidence of the absence of a single market within the EC. Although the traditional function of collecting customs duties was eliminated with the abolition of intra-EC tariffs, border controls remain necessary because of the differences in laws and regulations between member states.

Perhaps the most important function carried out at the border is ensuring that the correct indirect taxes accrue to the member states and preventing tax fraud and evasion. There is a system of tax remission and assessment so that the value-added and excise taxes, which vary considerably from one member country to another, are applied at the rate of the country the goods are entering to minimize competitive distortions. Border authorities also ensure conformity with the different health controls on a lengthy list of plant and animal products and make adjustments in agricultural product prices in accordance with the Common Agricultural Policy. In addition, a number of items are subject to import quotas in individual member states, and these must be regulated at the border. Finally, member country border controls have become increasingly important in a number of "new" fields: in combating drug traffic and terrorism and controlling the movement of non-EC citizens, particularly in connection with the sharp increase in illegal immigration and asylum seekers in recent years.

Not surprisingly, the result of these controls is delays—and costs—for road transportation. According to a 1984 study, trucks were held up at the internal EC-frontiers an average of 80 minutes at an estimated average cost of $36–$48 per hour.[1] A more recent report estimates the costs of formalities and delays at the frontier at almost $10 billion annually (equaling about 2 percent of intra-EC trade), in addition to at least $5.5 billion of forgone trade.[2]

(2) Limitation on Freedom of Movement of People and Their Right of Establishment

With the exception of certain transitional arrangements relating to Portugal and Spain, member country citizens have full freedom to move to another member state for work, whether employed or self-employed. The social security systems of the EC members are coordinated so that benefits can be transferred from one country to another. However, there is no such coordination among private benefit schemes, and that clearly represents a barrier to movement. EC citizens wishing to move to another member state for other than occupational reasons must obtain the permission of the government concerned.

The principal obstacle to the free movement of people within the Community has been the conditions placed by most member countries on the recognition of academic degrees and professional qualifications acquired in another country. An EC citizen has often found it difficult to transfer his or her professional skills to another member state as a result of obstacles reflecting concerns over the level of education and training and of their type and quality, the degree of enforcement exercised over the system, real or imagined differences in national customs and practices, and/or a desire by professional groups to limit "outside competition." Although difficult to quantify, this situation is probably more prevalent in the economically advanced northern EC countries vis-a-vis citizens from the less developed EC areas.

Whatever the reasons, observers report strongly "corporatist" and protectionist attitudes among professional groups in many member countries. This is perhaps not surprising when one considers the economic advantages derived by groups such as French architects and Italian notaries from the monopoly powers granted them under national law. For many professionals wanting to work in other member states, hurdles in the form of training and examinations are frequently present, although perhaps not as blatantly as in the assertion that an accountant in the EC would probably need to spend 50 years qualifying before being able to practice in each of the member countries.[3]

(3) Different Indirect Taxation Regimes

The Commission considers the differences in indirect tax regimes among the member states to be a major impediment to the establishment of an integrated market. These different taxes, unless regulated at the border, bring about competitive distortions as customers seek lower taxed products. At present, with the exception of cross-border shopping, which is considerable and is regulated bilaterally only to some extent, the taxes paid in the country from which goods are being exported are remitted, and the taxes are then applied by the country into which goods are imported. Thus, to a large degree, competitive differences are neutralized.

The two main forms of indirect tax that are addressed in the White Paper are the value-added tax and the excise tax. Although the member states agreed in 1967 to phase out their differing indirect tax systems in favor of a general application of a VAT system and followed this with agreement on a common basis for assessing the VAT in 1977, the national VATs are substantially different regarding the number and the level of rates and the coverage. Two member states (Denmark and the United Kingdom) apply one rate; the others have two or three. Two member states (Ireland and the United Kingdom) also exempt a significant number of items from the VAT. Apart from that category, the rates on different items range from 1 percent in Belgium to 38 percent in Italy, while the average VAT varies from 12 percent in Luxembourg and Spain to 25 percent in Ireland. Finally, the contribution of VAT receipts to government revenue as well as the ratio of VAT to GDP differ sharply among the member states. In terms of overall indirect taxation, the ratio of receipts to government revenue varies in eight EC countries, from 9 percent in Italy to 44 percent in Ireland (1984 data).[4]

On the other hand, the coverage of excise taxes is reasonably uniform (mainly on tobacco products, alcoholic beverages and mineral oils), but the rates vary widely, considerably more than in the case of VAT. For example, the tax on beer ranges from

0.03 European Currency Units per liter in France and Spain to 1.13 ECU in Ireland, while the spread on a packet of cigarettes extends from 0.12 ECU in Spain to 2.76 ECU in Denmark (1986 data).[5] In many cases this reflects a national government policy to promote the consumption of locally produced products—a phenomenon that becomes evident from an examination of the differences among excise tax rates on alcoholic beverages.

(4) Lack of a Common Legal Framework

To a considerable extent, the operation of enterprises in the EC is governed by national, rather than Community, laws and regulations. While initial harmonization measures have been adopted in certain areas—for example, in accounting requirements and product liability—there are no provisions for EC-wide enterprises other than the European Economic Interest Grouping, a limited type of small-to-medium sized joint venture. Thus, mergers, joint ventures and other forms of cross-border business activity are more complicated and difficult than they would be in an integrated market. For example, it is not possible to form a single corporation with registered offices in other member states.

Similarly, in the field of intellectual property, progress has been limited: trademarks are still issued on an individual country basis; patents are also issued nationally, although they can be obtained through a central EC office; and there are no EC-wide copyright provisions. Finally, the treatment accorded enterprises in member states varies according to the different nature and degree of enforcement of the relevant national laws and regulations.

(5) Controls on Movement of Capital

The Treaty of Rome provides that all restrictions on the movement of capital among member countries will be progressively phased out. It also includes "safeguard provisions" permitting member states to introduce "protective measures" in the event of disturbances in the capital market, although for limited periods of time and with Community authorization.[6] The countries using such measures do so because of the weakness of their currency and underlying economic policies, particularly as manifested in budgetary deficits and national debt.

Although there has been considerable progress in reducing the barriers to the free movement of capital among the member states—in France and Italy most recently—the situation remains mixed. In four of the countries (Denmark, Germany, the Netherlands, and the United Kingdom), unrestricted movement is permitted; four (Belgium, France, Italy, and Luxembourg) exercise some degree of control; and the remaining four (Greece, Ireland, Portugal, and Spain) maintain significant restrictions. To a large extent, long-term investment capital flows freely within the Community; the controls still in effect relate essentially to short-term movements of capital and activities of individuals.

(6) Regulation of Services

The service sector in the member countries is, on the whole, highly regulated by national governments. This is particularly the case with financial services (banking, insurance, brokerage, and securities), where the key issue is member states' exercise of control over and limitation of the right and conditions of establishment, especially for banks and insurance companies. In addition, EC governments regulate these institutions' activities and financial stability requirements in ways that normally vary from country to country. As a result of these regulatory regimes, the prices for financial services differ considerably among the member states, often by more than 50 percent, with the greatest margins in automobile insurance, home loans and consumer credit and securities.[7] According to an EC study, the potential gains from integration of the EC financial service sector is $26 billion.[8] Such estimates, of course, presuppose the successful liberalization of capital movements so that money can flow across borders to take advantage of the services offered.

Other service areas are also subject to considerable regulation. This is the case for all forms of transportation, including trucking which is subject to burdensome national quotas and other restrictions (over 50 percent of cross-border trips are rationed by bilateral permits negotiated between member states),[9] and air transportation, for which costs per ton and per mile are 50 percent higher than in the United States.[10] The same is true for television and other forms of broadcasting. This heavy hand—or heavy hands—of regulation has reduced the efficiency of the EC's service sector and retarded its development, particularly in the rapidly evolving areas affected by the revolution in information technology.

(7) Divergent Regulations and Technical Standards

In many respects this is the most complex area, and it is critical for the establishment of an integrated market, particularly in the case of high technology products and services. At issue are technical *standards* developed by private bodies in the EC, which in a formal sense are voluntary but in fact often assume quasi-mandatory status because of government action or commercial reality; *regulations*, or legal requirements laid down by governments, that often include such technical standards; *testing* procedures; and *certification* that the product conforms to the regulations and/or standards. The extent to which member countries have developed their own standards varies considerably, with some countries having highly developed and extensive systems. The three main national standards groups are AFNOR in France, DIN in Germany and BSI in the United Kingdom, and these are widely used by firms in other countries. However, throughout the EC, as in the rest of the industrialized world, a vast array of regulations and technical standards has been developed. The differences among them reflect historical patterns, domestic interests, philosophies on the role of government, and safety and consumer protection concerns. Needless to say, some of them are also protectionist in design and/or effect.

Unless the myriad of different regulations and standards can be brought under control, it will not be possible for the EC to develop an internal market of 320 million people and thus achieve the interaction and economies of scale that will enable it to compete satisfactorily in the global market. The costs of nonharmonization of regulations and standards are staggering: according to one estimate, almost $6 billion in the case of telecommunications, over $1 billion for foodstuffs and $3 billion for building products.[11] Some uniformity of standards has been achieved in the private sector Europe-wide standards bodies as well as by the Community, but to a large extent manufacturers are guided by national, rather than Community, provisions. A considerable effort has taken place to develop EC-wide standards, but the results have been meager.

(8) Public Procurement Policies

As elsewhere in the world, procurement by public authorities—in the form of supplies and public works—is big business in the EC, reflecting the significant role played by government in the member countries. Estimates of the size of this market vary, ranging as high as over $600 billion and accounting for 10 percent if not 15 percent of the Community's GDP.[12] Although a significant share of the above figures is accounted for by what would normally be considered local purchases by local authorities (noncompetitive bids, nontradable items and small quantities), they nonetheless include an enormous volume of "big ticket" items that could be supplied from outside the country, or the Community, at lower cost (as much as $400 billion, as estimated by one EC source[13]). According to a 1987 EC report, only about 2 percent of public contracts are awarded to firms in other member states and about 75 percent of contracts are awarded to "national champions" for whom the tenders are tailor-made.[14]

One factor contributing to the closed public procurement market is the exemption from application of EC public procurement regulations given to four sectors—energy, telecommunications, transportation, and water supply—a decision taken because of the mixture of public and private ownership and control in the different countries. In any event, the EC decisions on public procurement in the 1970s and the 1984 recommendation to open up bidding on public telecommunication contracts have proven ineffective. The most serious and frequent infringements of EC procurement regulations listed in a recent EC report provide a clear picture of the EC public procurement market: failure to publish invitations to tender; misuse of exceptional bid award procedures; bid conditions incompatible with legislation; unlawful exclusion of tenderers; discrimination in the evaluation of tenderers; and discrimination in tender awards.[15]

The net result has been massive inefficiencies inside the Community. The EC has estimated that savings from an open public procurement system would amount to $21 billion and that, over time, it would reduce the number of manufacturers and unit costs substantially in a number of industries—for example, boilers from 15 to 4 (20 percent cost reduction) and electric locomotives from 16 to 3 or 4 (13 percent cost reduction).[16]

NOTES

1. "Checks and formalities relating to intra-Community trade in goods," COM(84) 134, April 11, 1984, p. 6 (based on 1982 data).

2. Paolo Cecchini, *The European Challenge 1992* (Wildwood House, Aldershot [U.K.], 1988), p. 8.

3. "Creating a Single European Market," speech by Lord Young (British Secretary of State for Trade and Industry), Royal Institute of International Affairs, London, December 2, 1987.

4. *Fiscal Harmonisation: An Analysis of the European Commission's Proposals* (London: Institute for Fiscal Studies, 1988), p. 45.

5. Ibid., pp. 36 and 41. The ECU is a basket of 10 member state currencies (Portugal and Spain are not included), weighted in accordance with the country's economic strength, which serves as a unit of account in the Community.

6. Treaty of Rome, Articles 67 and 73.

7. Cecchini, *European Challenge*, p. 40.

8. Ibid., p. 37.

9. "Europe's Internal Market," *The Economist,* July 9, 1988, p. 34.

10. Ibid., p. 15.

11. Cecchini, *European Challenge*, pp. 25–26.

12. The high figures are those of Cecchini, ibid., p. 16.

13. Ibid.

14.   "Second Report from the Commission to the Council and the European Parliament on the implementation of the Commission's White Paper on completing the internal market," COM(87) 203, May 11, 1987, p. 16.

15.   "Proposal for a Council Directive coordinating the laws, regulations and administrative provisions relating to the application of Community rules on procedures for the award of public supply and public works contracts," COM(87) 134, July 1, 1987, pp. 1–2.

16.   Cecchini, *European Challenge*, p. 22.

The Outlook for 1992 $\boxed{4}$

One could conclude from a brief review of the White Paper that it is merely a compilation of long-existing objectives—and in many cases long-existing proposals—that have been repackaged. Even though that is true to some extent, it is more accurate to view the White Paper (and thus the formal program to complete the internal market) as a qualitative change, a document representing a unique undertaking whose whole is greater than the sum of its parts. One commissioner has referred to it as "a great notion . . . capable of capturing the imagination of a people and transforming the political and economic landscape."[1] If this comes to pass as envisaged, he may well be right.

The significance of the White Paper lies both in its comprehensiveness and its timetable. The authors wisely determined that far greater pressure could be applied on the decisionmakers if there were a public, and recognized, set of dates by which specific actions were to be taken. Not only is a detailed list included in the White Paper, but the Single European Act states explicitly that "the Community shall adopt measures with the aim of progressively establishing the internal market over a period expiring on 31 December 1992." Since the act was signed by all member governments, ratified by their parliaments and even approved by referendum in two countries, the degree of commitment is far greater than that resulting from a simple hortatory declaration. As a further means of applying pressure on the decisionmakers, the Commission publishes a report to the Council and Parliament every spring describing progress (or lack thereof) over the previous year,[2] and at the end of 1988 it will issue a "mid-term" report assessing developments over the first half of the eight-year period scheduled for completing the internal market.

Equally important, as indicated above, the White Paper covers the entire range of measures deemed necessary to complete the internal market. Despite the White Paper's comprehensiveness, the Commission downplayed proposals necessitating budgetary outlays or explicitly touching the key attributes of sovereignty, thereby enhancing the document's acceptability to the member states.[3] Another important element has been the Commission's steadfast insistence that the program is an inseparable whole. There cannot be "Europe a la carte," it asserts, wherein member states choose those parts of the White Paper they are prepared to adopt, because this would weaken the integrity of the program and necessarily risk gutting the internal market effort. Although progress has been, and will continue to be, uneven, the Commission's efforts have succeeded in preventing serious backtracking.

RESPONSES TO THE LAUNCH

By any measure, the outward manifestations of support for completion of the internal market are strong and pervasive throughout the Community. Virtually every member government has taken steps to publicize the program and to prepare its citizenry for the changes that will take place. Most visible has been France, where an extensive and comprehensive program of information has been undertaken, with the result that the level of public knowledge is probably higher there than elsewhere in the EC.[4] Similarly, the British government launched a publicity campaign in the spring of 1988 to increase private sector awareness from around 25 percent to 90 percent by the end of the year. As part of the formation of its new government in 1988, Belgium now has a "Secretary of State Europe 1992," who is responsible for explaining to the Belgian business community and public what the internal market program means for them and how best to prepare for it.

But member governments see not only a responsibility to make their citizens aware of the forthcoming changes, but also an opportunity to bring about needed changes in their domestic economies. The Chirac government, for example, apparently hoped to use the pressures created by the 1992 program to modernize and restructure the French economy, in part by doing away with archaic laws. Such an undertaking would have been far more difficult in the absence of the EC's internal market program. Similarly, some elements in the less developed southern member states hope that the process of completing the internal market will force much needed—and potentially far-reaching—changes in the legal structure, government administration and conduct of business in their country.

The EC private sector has perhaps been even more positive in its response and has supplied much of the pressure for carrying out the program. For example, whereas French and Italian industry strongly opposed removal of the intra-EC tariffs in the 1960s out of fear they would not be able to stand up to the foreign competition, they now solidly support establishing the integrated EC market. All national industrial federations have undertaken programs to inform their members about the various proposals and their potential consequences. Individual firms are looking more and more closely at the implications of an integrated market and are acting as if this will become a reality—which in itself accelerates the process.

Business leaders are speaking out increasingly, and often in stark terms, in support of completion of the internal market. One Italian business leader asserts "a unified Europe is no longer an option . . . but a necessity," while a leading industrial association refers to 1992 as "the last chance for Europe to meet the challenge of the international market."[5] The optimism within Community business sectors is quite remarkable. For example, a German poll in early 1988 showed that 90 percent of German firms expected the opportunities to outweigh the risks; in a 1987 survey of French business leaders, 78 percent expected completion of the internal market to benefit French industry and 65 percent expected it to benefit their own firms; and 8 out of 10 company directors polled in France, Germany and the United Kingdom considered the EC's program a positive development for their country's industry.[6] However, these polls are hardly definitive, especially as they apparently concentrated on the upper echelons of the business community. Private sector concerns clearly exist; these are normally couched in terms not of opposition but of calls for some form of protection.

For the Community's average citizen, "1992" is becoming increasingly recognizable and is frequently being used to refer to the program to complete the internal market.

All these actions and responses have been translated into a strong political consensus in favor of completing the internal market. Indeed, the program has assumed the status of a "motherhood" issue, virtually immune from political attack. It is rare and difficult for a mainstream politician to voice doubts about the integrated market program, for it is bad politics to be seen in opposition. In fact, a number of politicians have decided that an activist, pro-1992 stance can be a good means of attracting notice and advancing their own political ambitions.

One result of this consensus is that whereas in the past at any particular moment one member government or another seemed to be facing an election, which made it difficult for it to contemplate a decision on a thorny EC issue, political parties are now more likely to stress their devotion to the internal market cause. Thus, in France's 1988 presidential election, the main candidates vied with one another in asserting their ability to lead the country to "1992"; the British Conservative Party's 1987 election manifesto boasted of its successful handling of the recent British EC presidency in making progress on the internal market; and the new Italian government introduced a program to Parliament in 1988 liberally laced with references to "1992."

However, it would be misleading to imply anything like unanimous support for the single internal market. Behind the verbiage lie differing levels and intensities of concern. These sometimes take the form of opposition to specific measures or proposals from those, as is not surprising, who fear they would be adversely affected. The national customs officials who face prospective layoffs, the telecommunication employees of the highly protected national authorities and those connected with the host of enterprises benefiting from a protected market all have reason to view 1992 with less than unbridled enthusiasm, and they can be expected to make their influence felt with the decisionmakers.

But the concerns go beyond specifically affected individuals and groups. There is a strong tradition of protection—of markets, manufacturing and service sectors and enterprises—in many EC member states. While the French proclivity for protection of domestic economic interests is well known, it is less widely recognized that German liberal trade policy is a facade behind which important segments of the economy are subject to substantial regulation and regimentation. In many respects, then, the prospect of opening up hitherto sheltered markets, as is intended by the White Paper, is cause for considerable unease in the Community.

Whatever the opposition, however, by mid-1988 the internal market program had clearly acquired momentum. Just six months earlier, observers had debated whether the program would even get off the ground. As a Commission official recently put it, "we had been pushing the ball uphill for a long time, but now it's going downhill and the only question is the angle of the slope."

CAUSES FOR MOMENTUM

Even though the shift from uncertainty to certainty about the take-off of the internal market program was unexpectedly swift, the factors that played a role were reasonably clear. First, and of fundamental importance, was the establishment by the Single European Act of majority voting in the Council, which provided a mechanism for overcoming the obstacle to Community decision-making posed by the unanimity rule. As discussed in Chapter 2, the new system is still in the "breaking-in stage" as the EC institutions adapt to the changes, but it will no doubt force decisions in many previously blocked areas.

Second was a resolution of the problems of budgetary shortfall, which had hung over the Community during much of the early to mid-1980s. These difficulties had served as a brake on the internal market process in two ways: they had monopolized much of the attention and energies of those involved in the operation of the EC; and they had limited the availability of resources for nonagricultural purposes. But at its February 1988 meeting in Brussels, the European Council agreed on medium-term solutions to resolve the budgetary impasse and on a doubling of "structural funds"—to about $120 billion—for the depressed EC regions in the 1989–93 period. This accord enabled Community and member government officials to turn to the longer-range objectives of the internal market and at the same time to dampen the fears of the less developed EC members that completion of the internal market would exacerbate regional disparities. The latter consideration was important in helping to ensure the consensus necessary for the success of the internal market program and in promoting the objective enshrined in the Single European Act of strengthening "economic and social cohesion" in the Community.

Third was the introduction of the concept of "mutual recognition" and its offspring "home country control." These came about as a result of recognition of the practical (and enormous) difficulties the EC had experienced earlier in attempting to legislate uniform EC-wide measures and the growing acceptance of the principle of deregulation. Indeed, one observer has asserted that the "1992 project is an adventure in deregulation."[7]

Mutual recognition, as the name implies, means that a practice, regulation or another form of control in one member state will be recognized as valid in the other countries, even if it does not conform to such controls there. Thus, for example, the professional qualifications of an Italian architect will be automatically recognized in Germany, as will a British product manufactured in accordance with regulations imposed by the British government. The EC's role will be limited to agreeing on regulations of a general oversight nature that establish minimum conditions with which all member states must abide. The same concept applies in home country control (discussed below), whereby the supervisory or regulatory agency in the country where the enterprise is established will carry out those functions irrespective of where the enterprise actually operates in the EC. The net effect of these concepts is to reduce the area over which EC-wide agreement will be necessary and thus to enhance the prospects for movement toward 1992.

The final reason for momentum, although impossible to quantify or date, was the all-important "psychological snowball" of an idea whose time had come. The internal market increasingly became a topic of discussion, more and more people came to believe that the EC should move toward an integrated market, indeed that such action was imperative, and enterprises began to "think 1992" and to act accordingly. Thus, the process fed on itself and ultimately attained momentum.

DIFFICULTIES AND UNCERTAINTIES FACING THE PROGRAM

However, momentum and enthusiasm obviously will not suffice to ensure the success of the internal market program. In fact, it must be clearly recognized that serious difficulties exist, as evidenced by the significant number of proposals or issues that have been unresolved after consideration by the EC for many years predating the White Paper. The issues or measures in question are complex and difficult to resolve—to quote a German aphorism, the devil is in the detail. Almost without exception they present problems for one or another country or group within it. Often the subject of contention is linked to other issues, with a different set of problems and interests. It is rare that a country will be obdurate simply because it objects to change; far more frequently, serious issues are at stake. The scope of these issues, and the political and economic linkages, are illustrated in the following examples.

- The effort to institute approximation of coverage and rates for value-added and excise taxes runs afoul of (a) opposition by member state legislatures and governments to any impingement of one of the main forms of national sovereignty, i.e., determining taxation policy; (b) the very practical financial difficulty of offsetting any reductions in tax receipts that in many cases would result (and often would be sizable); and (c) the opposition for reasons of social policy to a reduction in "sin taxes" on cigarettes and alcoholic beverages.
- Although the issue was ultimately resolved, the Commission's efforts to obtain member states' agreement on a phased elimination of restrictions on intra-EC road transportation (such as national quotas and limits on out-of-country trucking) met strong opposition, especially from Germany, for reasons only partly related to transportation policy. To complement its subsidization of the railroads, the German government has limited competition in road transportation through various protective devices. A politically powerful network of small transport firms has developed, benefiting from legislation on working conditions but facing a more onerous tax regime than in most other member states. Accordingly, the German government insisted that it would be unfair to expose the German trucking industry to competition from the other member states before the social legislation and tax regimes had been harmonized.
- Opening up the public procurement market to competitive forces would put at risk a number of enterprises, many pos-

sessing considerable political influence, and would affect significant levels of employment.

- Differences in climatic and health conditions, as well as in traditions, present problems in unifying animal and plant health regulations. It is no accident that the greatest backlog in internal market measures is in this area. Perhaps the most prominent difference in the health area is the absence of rabies in the British Isles, a situation the British government is firmly determined to maintain. Another example relates to plant controls, where Spain, a subtropical country more susceptible to certain diseases, finds some proposed regulations, presumably based on more temperate climates, provide insufficient protection.

In addition to clear-cut difficulties, a number of uncertainties will affect the success of the internal market effort. One is the relationship between Brussels (basically meaning the Commission) and the member states—this is the issue of national sovereignty. Over time, as the EC has moved toward an integrated market, the powers of the collectivity have increased, involving a shift in responsibilities from national governments to Brussels. To some degree, this is perceived as a threat by politicians and civil servants in national governments, as well as by part of the general public. In member states with decentralized systems of government—notably Germany—the concern presumably is compounded. As discussed in Chapter 2, this tension between Brussels and the member states is reflected in the reluctance of the Council (representing member state interests) to increase the executive powers of the Commission to the extent it desires, which has led to friction between the two and some criticism by the Commission of the Council.[8]

Only in a limited number of areas—taxation and monetary union are notable examples—are national sovereignty concerns clearly voiced. Beyond these, such concerns have been less of an impediment to the internal market program than might have been expected; there is, in fact, little evidence of national sovereignty being an issue as such. One reason appears to be the gradualist approach employed in moving toward the integrated market so that issues are seldom posed in terms of national sovereignty. Another is that the areas of Community responsibility have largely been established by treaty. Nonetheless, the issue remains close to the surface, occasionally springing forth, particularly as differences among member states are aired about the ultimate objectives of the effort to create a single market. Prime Minister Thatcher clearly raised some fundamental, and controversial, issues in her September 1988 Bruges speech, in which she criticized the effort to "suppress nationhood and concentrate power at the center of a European conglomerate."[9]

Another relevant factor is the mediocre performance of member states in implementing EC decisions. One recent study terms the nonimplementation of EC rules and regulations by member states "a rising tide . . . threatening a breakdown in the Community system if it is allowed to continue for much longer."[10] The number of cases of noncompliance brought by the Commission to the European Court of Justice has increased steadily, with the vast majority of rulings against the member states. In addition, there have been a significant number of follow-up complaints against member states subsequent to Court judgments. According to one count, the number of infringement proceedings under EC laws increased five-fold in the 1976–86 period.[11] The record of implementation varies considerably by member state. Italy, followed by France, is a major offender, in part a reflection of its cumbersome administrative system. In any event, the prospect of a sizable increase in the volume of EC internal market legislation is grounds for concern based on past performance, both in terms of member state implementation and the ability of the EC institutions to provide enforcement.

In discussing uncertainties, consideration must also be given to Commission personalities. Since 1985 the responsible commissioner, Lord Cockfield, has played a dominant role in the Community's internal market activities. As noted in Chapter 1, his single-minded efforts have contributed substantially to the progress achieved thus far. However, Prime Minister Thatcher has chosen not to re-appoint him when his four-year term expires at the end of 1988. Thus, another commissioner will see the program through the second half of the appointed period. The performance of that individual will be one factor determining the evolution of the internal market. The momentum has been achieved, however, and other leaders, notably Commission President Delors, re-confirmed in office at least through 1990, will give high priority to carrying on the program.

Another area of uncertainty is the distrust that exists among the member states, and this cannot be overcome simply by regulation and exhortation. It is somewhat of a north-south phenomenon, in which the more industrialized northern countries believe that the southern countries do not always play by the rules and are less conscientious about enforcement of Community decisions. Although this phenomenon is unquantifiable, it clearly exists and represents a deterrent to completion of the internal market.

Finally, account must be taken of the strong likelihood—if not near certainty—that there will be resistance in areas where competitive forces are unleashed and important groups or even national interests adversely affected. If the liberalization of financial services results in substantial layoffs (for example, in the over-staffed Italian banking sector), if the Commission's competition policy causes cutbacks in member government aid to depressed industry with attendant unemployment and social unrest, if development of the internal market brings about hostile takeover bids from companies in other EC member states (which is already happening) and, in a broader sense, if regional disparities widen and/or economic growth stops, opposition to efforts to complete the internal market can be expected.

MEASURING OVERALL PROGRESS

Measuring progress achieved thus far and forecasting developments in the coming years is a difficult task. To the extent there is any precise measure, it is a quantitative one. As of the end of 1987, the Commission had submitted proposals for about two-thirds of the subjects included in the White Paper, and action had been completed by the Council on about one-fourth of these. The most recent tally of June 30, 1988 (the end of the German presidency of the Council) shows 211 proposals made by the Commission and 91 adopted by the Council. The Commission expects to be only slightly behind schedule, with 90 percent of its proposals submitted by the end of 1988. The Council is farther behind. On a strictly arithmetical basis, its record is not very good, with action completed on about one-third of the items at nearly the half-way point in the program. However, when compared to the timetable set out in the White Paper (which provides for more actions to be completed toward the end of the period), the numbers are less disappointing.

Although a review of the numbers provides a general idea of progress, it is more meaningful—though more difficult—to make a qualitative assessment. In doing so, it is important to recognize that "completion of the internal market" is not an all-or-nothing proposition. While the White Paper calls for completion of action on all the items (now 285) by the end of 1992—which would enable the Community to announce that the internal market is "complete"—the program is necessarily an evolving process. As one observer put it, "1992 is a process, not an event." Action will proceed at varying paces on the different issues, depending on their intractability and the strength of the political forces involved.

Despite the exhortations and efforts of the Commission—and of the treaty obligation contained in the Single European Act—the likelihood is remote that the EC will complete action on all measures in the White Paper by the end of 1992. The process will continue beyond 1992. Indeed, it is unlikely that a specific point will be identifiable at which the internal market becomes "complete." Rather, the yardstick will be how far the Community has proceeded from its situation at the outset of the program in 1985. In any case, the EC of 1992 is likely to be considerably different from that of 1988 and certainly that of 1985.

In making a qualitative judgment on progress toward the single integrated market, assessing the relative importance of various categories of measures is essential. From the outset, the Commission has consciously avoided setting priorities, as noted above, as part of its tactic of pressing for acceptance of the entire White Paper program. However, even though all measures will contribute to the objective of completing the internal market, it is relevant to identify the key areas:

- Elimination of border controls. Apart from the not inconsiderable costs, the psychological effect of the maintenance of physical frontiers is enormous.
- Opening up of public procurement. The share of economic activity affected is massive as are the cost savings and economic transformation that could take place as a result of government action.
- Harmonization of technical regulations and standards. This is essential to the ability of companies throughout the EC to rationalize and compete internationally, especially in high technology products.
- Liberalization of capital movements and the related liberalization of financial services. Once any individual or institution can move funds anywhere inside the Community and use any financial services offered, a major step will have been taken in the establishment of an integrated market.

ACTIONS ON AND PROSPECTS FOR 1992 MEASURES

Having reviewed the factors that will affect the efforts of the Community to remove the obstacles to an integrated market, it is now appropriate to examine the individual categories of barriers.

(1) Border Controls

It should be noted at the outset that border controls is the only barrier that does not exist for itself but rather to carry out other policies of the EC or, more frequently, those of the member states. Once the national policy differences have been sorted out—and not before—the border controls can be eliminated.

A major breakthrough in simplifying border controls took place with the introduction on January 1, 1988 of the Single Administrative Document. As the name implies, this form will substitute for the numerous forms (as many as 100, according to one count[12]) required by the member governments at the border and will serve as an export declaration, transit document and import entry. While some "teething" problems have been reported, the document should significantly reduce the time and cost of physical border controls. At the same time, the EC introduced a common tariff nomenclature, called the Community Tariff, that will be adopted by all member states and should also simplify border procedures.

These are, of course, only a beginning because they still involve paper transactions at the border and thus do not eliminate controls. The next step would be to institute a system of electronic (rather than physical) documentation for any necessary controls. This would obviate, or at least reduce, the need to maintain border controls, requiring instead a common system among the national authorities of the member states so they could "talk" to each other.

Many—but by no means all—of the border controls on freight traffic relate to the fiscal discrepancies among member countries. Controls are carried out at the frontiers to ensure that the VAT and excise taxes of the importing country have been paid to avoid competitive distortions, particularly in cases where taxes differ sharply in contiguous countries (such as Denmark-Germany and Ireland-United Kingdom). Prospects for the early introduction of a common taxation system that would eliminate the need for such controls are poor (see section 3 below). However, these controls could at least be reduced through the electronic system mentioned above, combined with supervision in the importing and/or exporting country. There is apparently considerable work under way, both in the private sector and the Commission, on developing such a system. But the results thus far have been limited, and the Commission's efforts on taxation have been concentrated on achieving agreement on tax harmonization.

The other main "traditional" area of border control activity, plant and animal health, presents considerable problems. Of the 285 White Paper measures, about 70 relate to this area, and it is primarily here that the Commission has been behind schedule in submitting proposals to the Council. The lack of progress has been the result of several factors: the differing sanitary situations in the member states; the sheer volume of different member country regulations needing to be harmonized; the technical nature of the regulations, which makes political decisions difficult; the insufficiency of administrative resources in the Commission; and the low priority given this area by national authorities. As the Community comes to grips with these issues, it may seek ways to permit the continuation of some differences among member states. Particular arrangements could be established for noncontiguous territories—in other words, applying different regulations for Greece, Ireland and the United Kingdom—or certain countries could impose different regulations (as they are permitted under the Single European Act) on the basis of health, safety and environmental considerations, as long as the government can prove that they do not represent arbitrary discrimination or a disguised restriction on trade. Nonetheless, in these cases the need for border controls would apparently remain.

As efforts are undertaken to remove the traditional causes for the maintenance of internal border controls, other requirements for border control have become increasingly prominent. These new issues—immigration, drugs and terrorism—present difficult problems. Unfortunately, one cannot expect a "victory" against drugs or terrorism by 1992, and thus there is strong pressure to maintain a physical presence at the frontiers to combat these problems. Although it is questionable whether border controls have proven, or could prove, an effective bar to drug and terrorist traffic—and here the U.S. experience may be instructive—there is clearly an emotional, psychological attachment in the member states to continued controls at the borders for this purpose. More serious for the Community is the problem of controlling immigration—a new phenomenon for the EC—which involves refugee issues as well as claims on national social security systems. A further complicating factor is the participation by Denmark in a passport union with the other Scandinavian countries (citizens of the latter can enter Denmark without a passport and thus in the absence of intra-EC border controls would be able to move freely inside the other member states).

Prospects. Although there will be considerable focus on the effort to eliminate border controls, because of their symbolic and psychological importance the issues that would have to be resolved to do so are particularly complex and controversial. Under the circumstances, some diminution of the extent of border controls and—most important for business—some reduction in the cost of trans-border shipment can be expected. However, elimination of border controls is highly unlikely by the end of 1992.

(2) Limitation on Freedom of Movement of People and Their Right of Establishment

Although nonprofessionals enjoy the ability to move to other EC countries to work, the acceptance of academic and professional qualifications acquired in a different member state has been a contentious issue. Efforts to negotiate directives on a profession by profession basis were undertaken prior to issuance of the White Paper, and some success was achieved, particularly in the health sector (for example, a directive covering physicians came into effect in the mid-1970s).

While work continued on some of the individual sectors, the White Paper called for a "framework directive" that would provide a general system to cover all professions. The main elements were to be acceptance of the principle of comparability of university studies among member states and mutual recognition of degrees and diplomas. Thus, although some directives on specific professions were adopted, notably on architects after 17 years of negotiations, work continued on the more general approach.

Despite the requirement for a unanimous Council vote (this being one of the areas not covered by the qualified majority provisions of the Single European Act), a breakthrough was achieved in June 1988. A directive was adopted that provides for the mutual recognition of professional qualifications; a university degree acquired in one state will be considered the equivalent of one in any other state. No distinction will be made on the basis of number of years studied or course of instruction. The principal exception is for all legally related professions (such as lawyers, accountants and patent agents)—as a result of strong pressure from that sector—and requires six months' study or an examination in the "receiving" country. Furthermore, proof of language proficiency will be required in some cases. This directive, which enters into effect in 1990, supersedes the more complex sectoral agreements previously adopted.

The only area still not covered by EC action is the so-called vocational professions, such as plumbing and masonry. However, the White Paper calls for measures to ensure the comparability of vocational certificates.

Prospects. The Council's action in June 1988 in large measure removed the remaining obstacles to the free movement of people within the EC. It is likely, however, that some resistance, largely informal and indirect but possibly quite effective, will be encountered, and thus the results will probably be somewhat mixed. While a certain movement of professionals can be expected from the less developed EC regions into the higher income ones, language and cultural differences will be limiting factors. An indication of the extent to which opportunities may be used is the fact that, during the first 10 years of the directive on physicians, only about 4,500 physicians out of an estimated EC physician population of 600,000 went to work in another member state.[13]

(3) Different Indirect Taxation Regimes

The Commission has placed high priority on harmonizing—or, more accurately, approximating—the main national systems of indirect taxes, VAT and excise taxes (although it recognizes other divergent indirect taxes, it considers these less relevant to the free movement of goods across borders).[14] In the fall of 1987, it took the first step by issuing a proposal for harmonization of VAT and excise tax regimes, and this has been the focus of intensive, often contentious discussion ever since.[15] In making this proposal, the Commission asserted that it was guided by two priorities: establishing the best possible fiscal environment for those participating in the market and minimizing the adverse effects of approximation on member state revenues and budget flexibility.

In drawing up its proposal, the Commission reviewed the U.S. experience with state taxes and decided not to seek a single, uniform system for the VAT because it believed this would be impractical to establish and unnecessary in preventing distortions of competition. Rather, it concluded, a spread of up to 5 percentage points would be essentially neutral in effect. Accordingly, its proposal calls for the member states to adapt their existing VAT to a two-rate system, with a standard rate plus a reduced rate for items of basic necessity. Countries would set their standard rate in the 14–20 percent range and the reduced rate between 4 percent and 9 percent. While recognizing the need for temporary derogations from the proposed rates, the Commission opposed maintaining zero rates (presently used in Ireland and the United Kingdom) on the grounds that they cause market distortions and that there are more efficient ways of achieving social policy objectives.

By definition, the VAT is a tax levied at each stage of production and distribution. Although it could have opted for a system under which the tax revenues remain in the member state of ultimate consumption, the Commission determined that it was important for the tax revenue related to activities in the exporting member country to accrue to that government. Thus, because the tax will in the end be collected in the consuming country, the Commission's proposal includes provision for a clearinghouse to apportion tax revenues in accordance with the location of the various stages of production and distribution.

Approximating excise taxes is more difficult because of the wide range of existing tax rates and because there is only one point of control (i.e., at the place of sale). Accordingly, the EC would either have to institute a single, uniform tax rate for each item or else devise a form of identification system to prove that the requisite tax had been paid. Seeking a system based on equity among the member states and a minimum of disruption in the sector concerned, the Commission opted for the first alternative. Its proposed list of taxes (specific for alcoholic beverages and mineral oils but ad valorem for tobacco products) is based in some cases on the arithmetic average of member governments' taxes, but in others on an attempt to maintain revenue neutrality.

Not surprisingly, the member states' reaction to the Commission proposals has been negative. Although most member states recognize the merits of some form and degree of tax harmonization, they consider two fundamental issues to be at stake. The first is that the power to levy taxes is one of the most basic attributes of national sovereignty. Even in the most fervently "European" member state, this is not a power that the government will yield lightly. It strikes at the heart of the formulation of economic policy, and until the Community moves much further toward a coordinated economic policy, governments will be unwilling to share that authority with Brussels.

The second reason is less philosophical and more immediate: the proposed changes would significantly affect the budgets of the national governments. The Commission noted in its proposal that 8 of the 12 member states' standard-rate VAT falls within the proposed range and that the proposed excise rates reflect a considerable measure of averaging. It then asserted that it would leave the primary task of calculating the effects of the proposed taxes to the member states. At the same time, however, it estimated that its proposals would result in a substantial increase in indirect tax revenue for Luxembourg, Portugal and Spain; an unchanged level of revenue for Belgium, Italy and the Netherlands; a slight budgetary loss for France; a small or moderate loss of receipts for Germany, Greece and the United Kingdom; and pronounced losses for Denmark and Ireland.

But even where the overall percentage shifts are small, they could have a disruptive effect on government revenue. Tax systems that have developed over time with a certain division between direct and indirect taxes, and among different forms of indirect taxes, cannot be easily altered. Offsetting a decline in indirect tax receipts by an increase in direct taxes, and vice versa, may present political problems and force reconsideration of basic economic policies. Many aspects of the national taxation systems have a strongly political content—for example, the exemption from VAT for children's clothing in the United Kingdom and the "luxury rates" on certain items in Italy. A prime ingredient of many excise taxes is the provision of incentives for the consumption of domestically produced alcoholic beverages and of "social taxes" on alcoholic beverages and tobacco products.

Thus far, the debate has been intense and progress minimal. Several member states have complained that the Commission's proposal would decrease their revenue. The French Prime Minister recently wrote that acceptance of the EC VAT average would "pauperize" the budget since it was politically impossible to increase direct taxation.[16] Luxembourg has calculated that the Commission's proposals on VAT and excise taxes would raise prices 7.5 percent and increase unemployment by 1 percent. Denmark has estimated that to recoup the revenue loss from adopting the Commission's tax harmonization proposals, it would have to increase income tax rates by 13 percentage points.[17]

Resistance in principle to tax harmonization has been strongest in the United Kingdom. While one U.K. private sector observer referred to the Commission's proposals as "a solution in search of a problem," the British government argued that it is inappropriate and unnecessary for the Community to harmonize indirect taxes—or, as the Chancellor of the Exchequer put it, the effort is "a bureaucratic non sequitur . . . a distraction from the issues to which we should really be devoting our energies."[18] In the government's opinion, member states will alter their tax rates as they deem necessary in response to the market pressures arising from the gradual abolition of border controls. This view is sustained in a recent study by the Institute for Fiscal Studies in London,[19] which asserts that differences in indirect taxes have little effect on business location or member state competitiveness and concludes that the Commission's proposals are aimed primarily at eliminating the need for border controls. Needless to say, this view is countered by those who assert that the marketplace cannot adequately bring about approximation of tax rates and that the ensuing adjustments would necessarily be downward, with adverse effects in many member states.

Prospects. It is difficult to foresee anything other than slow progress in harmonizing indirect taxes. The problems are difficult to resolve, and the national interests at stake are considerable. Thus, an EC-wide VAT and/or excise tax system in place by 1992 is highly unlikely. At best, there could be some movement, including somewhat greater flexibility for member states than the Commission has proposed.

(4) Lack of a Common Legal Framework

Many issues relating to the legal framework are the subject of long-standing and unresolved Commission proposals. However, the sharp increase in cross-border activity by EC and non-EC companies has added to the need for resolution of various outstanding issues.

In the area of EC *company law,* one accomplishment has been the adoption of a regulation in 1985 for European Economic Interest Groupings. Such groupings of up to 500 employees can be formed as of July 1989. Analagous to joint ventures, they will not be required to form new legal structures and will remain subject to the laws of the country of establishment. The purpose is to enable two or more firms in different member states to join forces on specific projects. The groupings represent the first example of a corporate body being established under EC law. In addition, the Commission proposed a directive in 1988 that would encourage the development of small business by offering sole traders limited liability through incorporation as a single-member company.

However, the main—and unresolved—issues of company law are contained in proposals for five directives. These cover harmonization of the structure of public limited companies, definition of the relationship between parent companies and their subsidiaries, facilitation of cross-border mergers, harmonization of financial disclosure requirements for branches of foreign (i.e., other member state or non-EC) companies, and harmonization of legal procedures relating to takeover bids. Consideration of the first three subjects predates the White Paper—the first one by over 10 years—and many contentious issues are involved, including those of social policy (see below). A further key issue is the proposed European company statute, which would provide rules for all aspects of company operations, as an alternative to member state law. Its main purpose is to enable groups in different member states to merge without having to adopt the corporate laws of either country. This proposal too has been stymied, primarily because of controversy over social policy.

A further set of issues relevant to the operation of firms relates to *company taxation*. In addition to special business taxes levied only in certain member states (such as the German Gewerbesteuer), there are significant differences among the member states in the base, rate and system of computation for corporate taxation. These differences not only affect the competitive situation but also create obstacles to cross-border activity in areas such as tax treatment of parents and subsidiaries, taxation on mergers and double taxation. As with other company law issues, the Commission proposals in these three areas predate the White Paper but have been included among the measures of the internal market program. However, unlike the others, taxation remains subject to unanimity in the Council, which adds to the difficulty of resolution.

There has been little progress with respect to *intellectual property*. A regulation was proposed in 1984 for the establishment of a Community trademark and a Community Trademark Office. Thus, firms would have the option (but not the obligation) of substituting a single trademark registration and protection for the existing 12. However, a protracted debate over where to locate the headquarters of the trademark office has prevented adoption of the regulation. Additional work is proceeding on a directive to approximate member state laws relating to trademarks.

Action is blocked in the case of patents as well. In a follow up to the European Patent Convention of 1973, a Luxembourg Convention was negotiated in 1975, providing for the establishment of a Community patent to be issued by the patent office (set up in Munich under the 1973 convention). The patent would have the same force in all member states, and the patent holder would thus not have to enforce his or her rights in each country. However, the ratification process of the Luxembourg Convention has come to a halt. Although seven member states have ratified the convention, constitutional problems have prevented two (Denmark and Ireland) from doing so, and the three most recent entrants to the EC (Greece, Portugal and Spain) have refused to ratify until presented with a document agreed to by the other nine. A decision was taken in June 1988 to hold an intergovernmental conference to seek a means of breaking the impasse.

Work is least advanced in the copyright area. At the end of 1986, a directive was adopted requiring member states to provide legal protection for microcircuitry, the first instance of harmonization of laws governing intellectual property protection. In June 1988, the Commission issued its long-awaited Green Paper (discussion paper), the first step toward legislation to harmonize copyright law in the Community.[20] It reviewed all areas of copyright law, including new technologies such as computer software, databases, microcircuits, and biotechnology, offering ideas on how to proceed and calling for suggestions from member states and other interested parties. The Green Paper included a detailed timetable for action and proposed to begin with submission of a measure for the protection of computer software.

Issues of company law have historically been intertwined with those of *social policy*, that is, working conditions, workers rights and social welfare. The White Paper (as indicated in Chapter 3), does not specifically raise issues of social policy, other than mentioning in passing, in the section on technical regulations and standards, that "the interests of all sections [of the economy] . . . should be incorporated in the policy on the health and safety of workers."[21] However, one issue of social policy clearly arises in connection with the proposals on company structure and the EC company statute—worker participation in management.

Any EC regime governing the structure of enterprises will have to take into account the existence of various forms of worker participation in management, the most extensive being the "co-determination" system in Germany, under which the larger firms are required by law to provide labor with one-half representation on their boards. Not surprisingly, Germany opposes any EC-wide scheme that would enable firms in Germany to avoid operating under the co-determination system. On the other hand, there is strong opposition to making worker participation compulsory in the EC not only because of philosophical views on the respective roles of labor and management but also because, on more practical grounds, this could put countries not used to such a system at a competitive disadvantage; further, in their view, the labor force in certain states would not use their newly acquired powers responsibly or would refuse to accept board seats. To resolve this conflict, the Commission has proposed that firms be permitted to choose from among three forms of worker participation, although all companies would have to observe existing national laws in the member state where the activities are carried out.

However, social policy issues extend well beyond company law. There has always been a line of thought within the Commission, and the Community as a whole, that the EC should undertake actions to protect and promote the interests of workers in the Community. Although this point of view has been quiescent for some time, it has gained greater prominence in recent months. In particular, Commission President Delors has expressed his conviction that the internal market program cannot be successful if EC workers believe it will operate against their interests. Accordingly, he has pushed for action on a "social agenda." This emphasis corresponds with the priorities established by the Greek presidency (second half of 1988), which will presumably be maintained by the succeeding presidencies of Spain and France.

The first step was the initiation, soon after issuance of the White Paper, of a series of meetings on social issues between the "social partners" (the representatives of EC employers and labor), termed the Val Duchesse dialogue. Then in its program for 1988,[22] the Commission stated its intention of moving ahead in the social policy area as set forth in the Single European Act. The act calls for improvements in worker health and safety, especially in the workplace, and an enhanced dialogue between labor and management. In the spring of 1988, the Commission adopted "guidelines" on social policy for EC action. These call for promoting improvements in working and living conditions, ensuring necessary conditions for the free movement of people, adopting conditions to enable workers to adapt to a single market, reducing social disparities and unemployment, and promoting an EC-wide dialogue between labor and management. The basic ideas of the Commission, contained in an internal working party report on the "social dimension," are intended to serve as the foundation for further discussion and action.[23] In effect, the Commission's initiative was endorsed at the European Council's June 1988 meeting, which "stressed the importance of the social aspects of progress towards the 1992 objectives" and that it was "necessary, besides improving working conditions and the standard of living of wage earners, to provide better protection for the health and safety of workers at their workplace."[24] Following that, the Commission issued a working paper setting forth its list of priorities and proposals for action.[25]

The political implications of the social policy debate are not clear. Although labor groups in the EC have voiced general support for the 1992 program in a number of statements, these have often been linked with expressions of concern over the implications for the Community's workers. As stated by a joint British-Irish union group, "the internal market represents a major challenge to trade unions"; the group called on the unions to link up internationally in response and to press for application of the principles of harmonization and freedom to operate for "the rights of workers and their terms and conditions."[26] One particular union concern is "social dumping," i.e., labor's fear that the integrated market will result in firms' shifting operations to areas with the lowest labor costs.

More directly relevant is whether labor's opposition or concern could stop or slow progress toward 1992. If it chose to do so, its most likely point of leverage would be the European Parliament, where it could influence the course of EC legislation. It should be noted that the members of Parliament face an election in 1989 and that the largest political group is the Socialists (who are more likely to reflect social concerns). Thus far, there has been little indication that EC labor is doing more than casting a wary eye on the process; however, its ability to impede progress on 1992 issues should not be discounted.

A final element affecting the operation of companies as the EC moves toward an integrated market is the Commission's role in *competition policy*. Proposals for carrying out enforcement of the Treaty's *antitrust* provisions (prohibition on mergers and takeovers likely to distort EC competition or give rise to a dominant position) have been the subject of discussion for about 15 years, when the Commission first requested authority to approve certain types of mergers and takeovers. Now, the urgency for action arising from growing cross-border activity has been combined with an increasingly active Commission determined to exercise its antitrust prerogatives.

Fortified by the 1987 Philip Morris decision of the European Court of Justice, which confirmed a broad interpretation of the

Commission's powers to approve mergers, the Commission has pressed member states to approve a proposal that would give it power to rule on significant cross-border mergers in advance. Apart from mergers of smaller firms and those largely limited to a single member state, the Commission would have to be notified in advance of a proposed merger (including those involving non-EC firms if there were a significant EC dimension to the merger). It would have two months in which to indicate the need for a review and the following four months in which to make a decision. The proposal would also give the Commission strong powers of enforcement: a fine of up to 10 percent of a firm's annual turnover for noncompliance with a Commission ruling.

The Commission estimates that 100–150 proposals would have to be notified annually and that only two or three mergers would be rejected or would require changes.[27] Although there is general recognition among member states of the need for such a policy, some have objected to the proposal because of the delays involved and concern over possible overlap between Community and national antitrust responsibilities (which may also be a cover for unhappiness over the possible loss of ability to prevent "unfriendly" takeovers from outside the member state).

Even though this proposal remains under debate, the Commission has flexed its enforcement muscles in the antitrust area, taking two significant actions in 1988. Early in the year, it negotiated for the first time with an EC firm over the terms of an acquisition—and forced British Airways to cede certain airport slots and routes in connection with its recent purchase of British Caledonian. Then in August it intervened for the first time before a merger had been concluded—in this case with a British consortium for allegedly contravening EC competition rules in connection with its bid for Irish Distillers. The Commission's authority was further strengthened by a European Court decision in September confirming its right to act against foreign-based firms violating EC antitrust rules on the grounds that the decisive factor is the place where the action takes place.

The scope for *state aids* by member governments to domestic industry is vast, encompassing measures from subsidies and concessional loans to subsidized research and development funds and debt write-offs. The Treaty of Rome states that aids that distort trade between member states or damage competing firms are illegal. However, certain forms of social aid are considered permissible, and exceptions are made for limited and clearly defined aid to regions or industrial sectors that is aimed at correcting regional imbalances or permitting struggling sectors to readjust.

Authority for enforcement of these provisions is given to the Commission, which requires member states to report intended state aids to it for approval. In recent years, member states have become more forthcoming in making such reports, with notifications rising from 124 in 1986 to 316 in 1987.[28] At the same time, the Commission has become more active in bringing member state practice into accord with the Treaty. In 1988, for example, it negotiated with the French government over the terms of Renault's capital restructuring, forced the British government to reduce substantially its proposed debt write-off for the Rover Group prior to its privatization, and required an Italian state holding company to recover an "illegal" $200 million payment it had made to a subsidiary to cover losses. During a four-year drive, the Commission forced EC member governments to reclaim about $1.2 billion in illicit state aid, with the greatest portion by far coming in 1987. In terms of developing general policy, however, the Commission has remained behind schedule. As of mid-1988, it had not made good on the undertaking in the White Paper to issue an inventory of state aid, intended to provide an overview of all state aid activity as a basis for policy formulation, and a report on implications for future state aid policy.

Prospects. The interrelationship between company law and social policy raises questions about the Community's ability to settle some of the outstanding issues in this area, and the increasing prominence given to social issues diminishes the likelihood that compromises will be found. Nonetheless, as political pressures rise for resolution of outstanding issues before 1992, it is possible that the Community will reach consensus on some company law issues, particularly if both labor and management can live with several permissible versions of worker participation.

In the field of intellectual property, the trademark issue is ripe for resolution and, despite the important consideration of national pride, it is likely that the headquarters issue can be resolved. On the other hand, the patent impasse appears more difficult to overcome; the most feasible course would be to "leave behind" the two countries with constitutional problems, though that would run counter to the principle of a unified Community. A good beginning has been made in the copyright area, but the issues involved are complex, and the development of specific proposals, and decisions on them, are likely to take some time.

With respect to social policy, there are three types of issues to be considered. Actions relating to working conditions, especially health and safety at the workplace, are most likely to be taken, with harmonization probably occurring at a reasonably stringent level. The issue of worker participation, deadlocked for so long, may well be resolved, although most likely in a way that essentially maintains the status quo of differing regimes. On the other hand, the more general social issues—such as workers rights, EC-wide collective bargaining and social benefits—are likely to be characterized more by rhetoric than action. There will be less compelling reasons to arrive at solutions and, indeed, less developed regions may prefer that none be reached to maintain the advantages they derive from lower labor costs.

Finally, with the Treaty and both recent and prospective Court decisions on its side, plus an active current leadership, the Commission is likely to expand its activist role in enhancing competition within the EC. This will clearly be a key factor in determining the success of the integrated market program. Agreement can be expected in the near future on the Commission's merger proposal. However, although the Commission will remain vigilant in the battle against state aids, many counterpressures will undoubtedly arise as competitive forces are unleashed, and the Commission will likely be forced to bend to some of them.

(5) Controls on Movement of Capital

In the White Paper, the Commission lists three aims for its capital liberalization policy: to increase the effectiveness of financial intermediaries and markets; to maintain monetary stability (working in parallel with reinforcement of the European Monetary System); and to promote the optimum allocation of savings by de-compartmentalizing financial markets. However, in carrying out that policy it has been obliged to take into account the differing levels of liberalization already achieved by the member states and the problems they have faced in moving toward completely free movement of capital.

Various liberalizing actions have been taken over the years by the member states, collectively and individually, including adoption of a directive in 1986 requiring the liberalization of capital movements in connection with long-term commercial transactions, bond issues and unquoted securities. In 1987, the Commission submitted an ambitious package of proposals designed to remove the last remaining barriers to the free movement of capital in the EC, including short-term monetary instruments, personal bank accounts and some types of loans. The proposal also provided for a fund for loans to member states encountering monetary difficulties resulting from the removal of restrictions.

These far-reaching proposals struck at the deep-rooted concerns of member states with actual or potentially weak currencies. First, they feared that hitherto "locked up" capital would leave the country, creating downward pressure on the value of their currency, and/or that there would be erratic capital movements and resultant sharp exchange rate fluctuations. In the case of Italy, for example, the public sector deficit is enormous—approximately equal to the annual gross domestic product—and virtually all of the national debt is held by Italians. Should such savings be offered alternative opportunities outside of Italy—with higher returns—there could be a significant outflow, with adverse effects on the value of the lira and the government's ability to fund its debt. Second, countries with relatively high tax rates, particularly Denmark and France, worried that their citizens would shift capital to countries, both inside and outside the Community, with lower tax rates to maximize their returns and avoid payment of home country taxes. This, of course, would be made possible by the absence of harmonization among member states' tax treatment of interest income.

In view of these very real concerns, it was a triumph of optimism that the EC agreed to a program of full capital liberalization in June 1988. The decision calls for the removal of any remaining barriers by mid-1990 in the eight more advanced countries and by 1992 in Greece, Ireland, Portugal, and Spain, with the possibility for a further extension for Greece and Portugal until 1995. A Community safety net was created in the form of a $20 billion loan mechanism for member states that experience balance of payments difficulties. Member states maintain the right to reimpose restrictions, subject to Commission approval; however, this authority will be reviewed in 1992. Although consideration had been given to maintaining some controls on capital flows to non-EC countries, capital liberalization was made universal, at least in part because it would have been difficult to enforce such a ban on the several member states already practicing full liberalization. To meet the concerns of Denmark and France, the Commission committed itself to developing proposals by the end of 1988 to deal with the risk of distortions and tax evasion arising from differences in member state taxes on interest, dividends and capital income; the Council pledged to act on these by mid-1989. Despite these commitments, it must be recognized that any decisions on taxation will not come easily because they will have to be taken under the rule of unanimity.

Although reinforcement of the EMS, as indicated above, was included among the Commission's aims, no specific action was taken in this regard as part of the capital liberalization directive. However, the European Council, at its June 1988 meeting, took the first tentative step in the direction of an EC central bank (as discussed in Chapter 5).

Prospects. The Council passed a major milestone in the program to complete the internal market by its courageous decision to phase out remaining controls on capital movements. Thus, full capital liberalization will formally be in place by the end of 1992 (with the not unlikely exception of the two least developed EC members). However, the key question is whether member states will find it necessary (or convenient) to reimpose restrictions—or to delay their relaxation. Judging from the threats that complete liberalization presents to the weaker currencies and the speed at which monetary flows can take place, it is quite likely that the path to complete liberalization will not be smooth and steady, but rather characterized by some backsliding. However, despite some observers' criticism of the safeguard clause—one asserted that it "would hang like a sword of Damocles above the tenuously unified internal market"[29]—it seems to have been a necessary precautionary measure. Although the safety net is provided, the Commission can be expected to be reasonably strict in granting permission for its use.

(6) Regulation of Services

The Commission views the service sector as critical because of its steady growth and future importance, in absolute and relative terms, in the EC economy. Indeed, the White Paper asserts "it is no exaggeration to see the establishment of a common market in services as one of the main preconditions for a return to economic prosperity."[30] To bring about this common market, the White Paper called for action in 22 areas; by early 1988, the Commission had submitted 17 such proposals, with the remaining five expected before the end of the year.

Much of the Commission's attention has been focused on financial services, an area characterized by rapid technological change (often leapfrogging national regulatory policies), the blurring of previously existing demarcations between different types of services and service industries (moving toward a single financial services industry), and a heavy degree of member state regulation (particularly at the retail level). The issues addressed in the White Paper relate essentially to the provision of services and the right of establishment.

In this area, the Commission has based its approach on four main foundations: (1) deregulation of operations, enabling financial institutions to move toward greater geographical scope of operations and greater range of services provided; (2) harmonization of the essential standards set by the member governments for prudential supervision and for the protection of investors, depositors and consumers; (3) mutual recognition among the member states of those standards; and (4) the radical principle of home country control—in other words, control and supervision of financial services by the authorities of the country in which they are based for all their EC operations, including those in other member countries.

In *banking*, following preliminary steps dating from 1977, the Commission submitted its proposed second bank coordinating directive for the establishment of an EC-wide banking system.[31] The proposal calls for a single license to be issued to a credit institution in its home country, but the institution would have the right to establish operations and provide services throughout the Community. The institution could offer any service permitted in its home country as long as that service is included in a list annexed to the directive. That list is drawn from a liberal universal banking model and includes all forms of transactions in securities. Thus, even if institutions in the receiving state cannot be offered the service, it can be offered by a bank from another state. The directive provides for home country control for all matters other than monetary policy, monitoring the liquidity of banks and the regulation of banks' security operations. Mutual recognition by other member states is made possible by the harmonization of essential rules, such as the level of initial capitalization, oversight over the identity and interests of the major shareholders, and limitation on the size of participation by the institutions in nonfinancial undertakings. A final provision, of direct relevance to the United States, is that single-EC banking licenses will be issued only to banks of countries in which reciprocal treatment is accorded banks of member states (see Chapter 7).

Two essential related issues concern harmonizing regulations on "own funds" and on the banks' solvency ratio. A directive was proposed in 1986 to harmonize the definition of the "own funds" of a credit institution; by mid-1988 it was close to adoption. The solvency directive, proposed in 1988, would establish the different risk categories of the institution and a minimum ratio of capital to risk-weighted assets; it is similar to proposals developed by the Bank for International Settlements.

The far-reaching proposal for EC-wide banking will be the subject of intense discussion. As envisaged, banking services will extend across member state borders to a far greater degree than hitherto, as will "competitive deregulation," under which member states will face pressure to remove restrictions on the operations of domestic banks because of competition from outside banks that provide services not permitted under national regulation. Success of the system will depend on mutual trust and close coordination among the member states' supervisory authorities.

In a related development, the Commission has been working toward a system of interoperability of *card payment systems*. The White Paper calls for the definition of common technical features of machines used to produce new payment cards and agreements among card issuers on the compatibility of systems, linkages and commission rates. In early 1987, the Commission made a number of proposals aimed at the development of the interoperability of payment cards through standardization and reciprocal interconnections throughout the Community. This included a code of conduct (since adopted) for the relevant European organizations to develop standards and consumer protection measures. A group of leading EC banks has developed an EC-wide system, although that has raised questions about the possible distortion of competition in connection with conditions of access to the system and market sharing. The Commission is reviewing this issue.

Two directives on *insurance* during the 1970s (predating the White Paper) facilitated the exercise of the right of establishment for general and life insurance companies and coordinated the rules and practices for supervision. In addition, the Council adopted directives in 1987 on credit and legal expenses insurance, which filled the gaps in the general insurance directive.

However, these were relatively insignificant measures in relation to the main issues of the 1980s, which involved the provision of insurance, particularly nonlife, across EC borders without establishment in the country where the services are provided. The European Court of Justice played a role (as described in Chapter 2), in a series of decisions at the end of 1986, by confirming the qualified right of a company in one member state to provide nonlife insurance in another country without being physically established there.

In a follow up to those decisions, the Council adopted a directive in 1988 that will coordinate nonlife insurance legislation on the basis of home country control. In meeting the argument that it is difficult for consumers to assess the quality of contracts and the soundness of the insurer, the directive removed the member state restrictions only for "large risk" customers, i.e., those deemed able to make the necessary judgments on their own (defined as firms above a specified size and also all transportation and merchandise trade). These firms can now purchase nonlife insurance from any authorized insurance company in the EC. However, protection is maintained in this area for the general public (the "mass risk" category) by requiring insurance to be written by firms physically present in the national market; similar provisions apply for all motor vehicle insurance. The Commission plans to submit proposals in 1988 on life insurance and third-party motor vehicle insurance (itself divided into large risk and mass risk categories). Life insurance will be deregulated in a number of stages. The final step would be complete home country control for mass risks, but that would require an extensive degree of harmonization.

Accompanying the development of financial services across member state borders have been efforts to develop uniformity and coordination of the operation of *stock exchanges*. This is an important area in view of the increasing popularity of equity investment and of competition among stock exchanges. In 1980 a directive was adopted that coordinates the requirements for the listing of firms on stock exchanges. This directive was amended in 1987 by provision for the mutual recognition of prospectuses. Also in 1987, the Commission proposed a directive on insider trading, intended to combat fraudulent use of privileged stock market information. With such legislation existing in only three member states, the directive would force the other member states to institute equivalent protection. Beyond that, however, a proposed directive is apparently being developed within the Commission to provide for a deregulated regime along lines similar to other financial services.

Another "traditional" service area is *transportation*, in which competition has been tightly controlled. Restrictions on water transportation—the most important being the prohibition on non-resident companies from engaging in inland service in another member country (cabotage)—is apparently not high on the priority list. On the other hand, removal of the burdensome restrictions on road transportation, which account for over 80 percent of goods carried across intra-EC borders,[32] was the subject of contention within the Community for a long time. However, it was agreed in June 1988 to phase out the quotas and other restrictions by the end of 1992.

Perhaps the most visibly restrictive transportation sector has been *civil aviation.* National carriers, with government support, have combined to institute a system of pooling of traffic, strict controls over the setting of fares and capacity, and limited access to the market. As any user of air services in the EC can attest, the result is remarkably high fares for intra-EC travel, although the effects have been mitigated by the establishment of extensive deep-discount and charter systems. The Commission has taken particular aim at this system, as a matter of transportation policy and of competition policy. Under considerable pressure from the Commission, including the initiation of proceedings against 10 carriers for infringement of competition rules, the Council adopted a package of four measures at the end of 1987. This represented the first step toward deregulation, in the form of agreement on the modalities for setting fares, weakening of the capacity-sharing regime and provision for increased market access. The Commission issued follow-up rules in mid-1988 designed to prevent anticompetitive agreements among airlines on fares, flights, computer reservation systems, and airport handling systems. Despite these developments, considerably more far-reaching measures will be required before the EC can achieve its objective of a common civil aviation policy.

The White Paper gives due emphasis to the *new technologies*, defined as audiovisual services, information and data processing services and computerized marketing and distribution services. It also stresses that an integrated market will require the installation of appropriate telecommunication networks with common standards. However, apart from developments on telecommunications (described in Chapter 8), which are not formally a part of the program to complete the internal market, there has been little progress.

The White Paper lists development of a single Community-wide *broadcasting* area as an objective and indicates the need to address areas such as limitations on advertising and the retransmission of broadcasts. In addition to undertaking a number of actions aimed at alleged infringements of the freedom of broadcasting by national authorities, the Commission issued a proposed directive on broadcasting in 1986, which was intended to establish a framework for regulation by providing for the approximation of member state laws in areas such as production and distribution of television programs within the Community, broadcast advertising and protection of children.[33] The Commission's goal is the establishment of a single market for television broadcasting to which all within the EC can tune in. However, there are a number of difficult problems caused by the mutual existence of public and private broadcasting, as well as contentious proposals for a ceiling on advertising time, restrictions on program content (sex and violence) and establishment of a quota for programs produced in the EC (60 percent has been mentioned as as an objective). Despite consideration of broadcasting by the Community, it is possible that the EC will be preempted by the Council of Europe (a 21-nation loosely organized regional body), in which work has progressed farther. In fact, some member states prefer that this forum be used rather than the EC.

Prospects. The Commission has unleashed a process of major change in the financial services area. While this represents a radical solution to the problem of how best to bring about a modern, efficient EC-wide industry—and therefore will cause misgivings and fears in many quarters—it is hard to imagine that the momentum for such change will be derailed. There may be obstacles to the Commission's proposals in such forms as pressures to maintain greater prudential protection and the difficulties of developing a coordinated system of supervision. However, the basic outlines of the program can be expected to be confirmed.

Passage of the banking directive in 1989 is likely, as is considerable progress by 1992 in the deregulation of insurance. In all these areas, including securities regulation, member states will promote their financial institutions' relative position in the Community—whether the U.K.'s desire to maintain London's position as the EC's predominant financial center, Germany's desire to centralize and expand the role played by its stock exchanges or Luxembourg's desire to maintain the advantages in its banking sector of low taxes and tight secrecy laws.

A start has been made in removing barriers in transportation. Although the principle of restriction-free road transportation has been accepted, one can expect many hurdles as a phase-out of quotas releases strong competitive forces. Similarly, the complete removal of the many restrictions among air carriers cannot be expected by 1992 because of the national interests and pride involved.

It is difficult to discern much activity in the new technologies area. The issues involved are controversial and not susceptible to rapid resolution.

(7) Divergent Regulations and Technical Standards

The White Paper places heavy stress on the obstacles to an integrated market presented by the different national product regulations and standards, both in terms of their direct effect on prices and of the many indirect inefficiencies and trade distortions. In so doing, it conceded that the system in place had proven inadequate. Under that system, instituted in 1969, approximately 200 directives were adopted establishing technical regulations. While these included some significant measures—such as the 1970 "low voltage" directive with its widespread application in the consumer electrical area—the results were minuscule compared to the annual establishment of about 5,000 technical standards by national standards bodies. The slow progress reflected the rule of unanimity in Council voting and the practice of setting out detailed specifications. With this background, the White Paper identified mutual recognition by member states of the regulations and standards of others as an effective strategy, supported by the Treaty of Rome provisions that prohibit national measures having the effect of restricting intra-EC trade.

However, the White Paper concluded that the exclusive use of neither the old system of full harmonization of member state regulations nor the adoption of the principle of mutual recognition would prove adequate. Accordingly, it announced a "new approach" to technical standards.

- Harmonization at the EC level (by Council decision) will be limited to "essential requirements," defined as those relating to health and safety and consumer and environmental protection. This means producing a broad statement of perhaps 10 pages rather than a detailed text of 150 pages, as in the past. Instead of listing complex specifications, the directive would indicate the required characteristics (e.g., the permissible degree of tilt of a tractor or the noninflammable nature of a toy rather than detailing how those characteristics are to be achieved).
- As long as member state authorities conform to these essential requirements, they can establish their own standards, which will be subject to mutual recognition by authorities in the other member states. These standards will govern until the next step is taken.
- European standards bodies will develop Europe-wide standards to the maximum extent. These private sector groups draw membership from the relevant industrial sectors and operate on a Europe-wide (rather than EC-wide) basis. The two most important bodies are CEN (European Standards Committee) and CENELEC (European Electrotechnical Standards Committee).

The White Paper then lists priority sectors for action: information technology and telecommunications, construction and foodstuffs.

A necessary adjunct to the new approach was reaffirmation in 1985 of the obligation contained in a 1983 directive for national governments to notify the Commission in advance of all draft regulations and standards concerning technical specifications. It provides for a standstill to be imposed on such national measures while a harmonized EC standard is being developed. This effort seems to have been successful, at least as measured by the increase in notifications by member states.

Despite adoption of the new approach, work is proceeding in the EC on the basis of both the old and the new approaches. Under the new approach, the first action was agreement on the essential requirements for simple pressure vessels in 1987, followed later in the year by similar action on toy safety. Other accomplishments in 1987 included two environmental measures harmonizing emission controls on large passenger cars and on commercial vehicles; remarkably rapid agreement on standards for cellular telephones (see Chapter 8); and completion of work on a package of measures relating to high technology medicinal products.

Further progress was achieved in 1988. This included a directive for the important building products sector and a series of directives fixing rules for food additives and packaging plus regulations regarding production, storage and distribution of frozen food. But the most important measure brought under consideration in 1988 was the engineering machinery directive, covering several thousand types of industrial machines that represent a turnover of about $240 billion. This proposed directive includes safety requirements and provides for specific standards to be developed over the next two years by CEN and CENELEC, with mutual recognition governing until then.

Some concerns have been expressed about the ability of the European bodies such as CEN and CENELEC to handle the sharply increased workload implied by the new approach on standards. In fact, the scope of their activities more than doubled in 1987, and the Commission provided additional funding to assist them in this effort.

Despite the obvious difficulties inherent in achieving a measure of EC-wide standardization, the mood in Europe is remarkably upbeat about the progress achieved thus far. In general, it is asserted that the main problem is the physical volume of work involved in reviewing a mass of technical material. Although concerns exist over possible attempts by one or another country with a highly developed standards system to impose that system on the rest of the Community (Germany, with its comprehensive and widely used DIN system, would be the most likely candidate), such concerns have been muted.

Nonetheless, the process of standards setting is hardly problem free. First, the shift in emphasis from drafting descriptive directives to listing aims has apparently been difficult for government officials. Reportedly one of the points of contention on the engineering machinery directive, for example, has been how much detail to include. Second, the Single European Act contains a clause permitting a member state, despite adoption of a harmonization measure on the basis of weighted majority, to impose its own (presumably more stringent) national standards on the grounds of "major needs" (defined, for example, as protection of health or protection of the environment), as long as the Commission confirms that the measure is not a disguised restriction on trade. Denmark has invoked this provision in connection with automobile emission standards, and other member states may do likewise. Irrespective of the merits of such actions, the net result is to perpetuate different standards in the Community. Third, it must be assumed that almost every case will require resolution of some conflicting interests, national or other.

Although progress has been achieved on regulations and standards, that has not been the case in the equally important areas of testing and certification. This is clearly the weak link in the progression of steps to bringing a product onto the market. The member state testing and certification bodies represent a mix of government and private organizations recognized by governments. The Commission would like to introduce the mutual recognition of testing and certification among these groups. This would involve establishing criteria for acceptable laboratories, a system for accrediting foreign laboratories and a code of good conduct for certification bodies. In many respects, this is a difficult task because of the extent to which the process, especially testing, relies on factors that cannot be easily defined, such as the individual skills of testers and their interpretation of data. To obtain input into the development of specific proposals, the Commission organized a large meeting of interested organizations in June 1988, which it hoped would help bring about a consensus on future policies. It was apparent at the meeting that the Commission is looking to a mutual recognition system organized on a sectoral basis and overseen by an EC body.

Prospects. It is hazardous to generalize about the future of regulations and standards in the EC. By all indications, the new approach is working reasonably smoothly—better than generally expected—and it is likely that directives will be adopted in a number of important areas. At the same time, regulations and standards have always been used to protect domestic interests, and there is no reason to expect such efforts to diminish. Nonetheless, EC enterprises will continue to benefit in many areas from the harmonization of standards; thus, the net result should be an increase in harmonization through the simplified procedure, resulting in some reduction in the obstacles to trade.

On the other hand, it is harder to be optimistic about testing and certification. Although the Commission is conscious of the key role these play—and recognizes that maintenance of restrictive national practices could negate progress on the harmonization of regulations and standards—the outline of a strategy to harmonize this area is not yet apparent. Any assessment, therefore, has to be guarded.

(8) Public Procurement Policies

Terming the fragmentation of the EC in the area of public procurement "one of the most evident barriers to the achievement of a real internal market,"[34] the Commission has undertaken an ambitious program to force changes in the Community's public procurement practices. Essentially it is seeking to accomplish two goals: extend the effective coverage and effectiveness of EC regulations, and improve the legal and administrative remedies for aggrieved parties and the Commission to redress evasion of these regulations. Action is taking place in four areas:

- Supply contracts. In March 1988, the Council adopted a directive covering supply contracts over ECU 200,000 ($240,000), aimed at ending abuses through closing loopholes in the existing directive. The directive, which becomes effective at the beginning of 1989, requires advertising in the EC's *Official Journal*, obligatory use of common standards and more effective monitoring and reporting.
- Public works contracts. Basically a parallel document to the supply contracts directive, the Commission's proposal is aimed at increasing the access of EC firms to tenders and thus expanding intra-EC competition. As of mid-1988, the directive, covering contracts valued above ECU 5 million ($6 million), was under discussion in the Council and Parliament.
- Excluded sectors. In June 1988, the Commission proposed a directive to extend EC-wide public procurement rules to the four previously excluded sectors (energy, telecommunications, transportation, and water supply). To avoid the problem posed by the mixed patterns of private and public ownership and control of industries in these sectors, the rules governing supply and public works contracts would apply to any purchasing authority that, because of its exclusive networks or concessionary rights under public control, would be unlikely to resist political pressure to "buy national."[35]
- Enforcement. A proposed directive is intended to attack the twin problems of insufficient redress for aggrieved parties and insufficient enforcement powers for the Commission. Under the proposal, member states would be required to make it possible for aggrieved parties to pursue judicial remedies to alleged wrongdoing (normally through the national courts), and the Commission would be granted increased powers to intervene to ensure that the proper procedures were being followed.

Prospects. It is difficult to overemphasize the strength of the economic, political and psychological forces that will oppose changing the status quo on public procurement. Such transactions represent a considerable share of the Community's GDP (as noted in Chapter 3), and the proposals of the Commission put at risk many strong local and national interests. They also run counter to decades-long traditions of local and national preference, which in many cases reflect economic and social imperatives. The Commission has made a good beginning, obtaining agreement on one measure—albeit the easiest—and laying on the table significant measures in the other three areas. It has wisely adopted the strategy of concentrating first on obtaining legislation and then on enforcement of the various measures. It has shown energy and determination. Nonetheless, progress is bound to be slow. Although the Commission may well obtain approval for most of what it has proposed by 1992, innumerable vested local and national interests are likely to fight to maintain a privileged position, depressed areas will look for special treatment, economic dislocation resulting from more open tendering will create political counterpressures, many purchasing authorities will try to ignore EC rules (more likely at the regional and local level), and the pursuit of legal remedies (a course of action many EC firms may be reluctant to follow) will be protracted. In sum, there will be more progress on paper than in fact.

NOTES

1. "External Aspects of the Internal Market," speech by Commissioner Peter D. Sutherland, Top Management Round Table Conference, London, February 22, 1988.
2. The three so-called implementation reports issued thus far are Commission documents COM(86) 300, May 26, 1986; COM(87) 203, May 11, 1987; and COM(88) 134, March 21, 1988.
3. Jacques Pelkmans and Alan Winters, *Europe's Domestic Market*, Royal Institute of International Affairs Chatham House Papers No. 43 (London: Routledge, 1988), p. 9.
4. For example, an unpublished study, "Europe in 1992," Ernst & Whinney, February 1988, concluded that a far higher percentage of French businessmen were aware of the internal market program (87 percent) than their British (38 percent) or German (35 percent) counterparts.
5. Carlo De Benedetti, "How to Make Europe More Competitive," *Wall Street Journal*, March 30, 1988, and the official position of the Lombard Industrial Association on the single European market, 1988.
6. "Verschaerfter Wettbewerb durch Europaeischen Binnenmarkt?," Association of German Chambers of Industry and Commerce (DIHT), Bonn, March 1988; and "Europe in 1992," Ernst & Whinney.
7. "Europe's Internal Market," *The Economist*, July 9, 1988, p. 8.
8. See 1987 and 1988 implementation reports.
9. "Emphasis placed on sovereign identity of European state," *Financial Times*, September 21, 1988.
10. Alan Butt Philip, *Implementing the European Internal Market: Problems and Prospects*, Royal Institute of International Affairs Discussion Papers 5 (London, 1988), p. 2.
11. "Defence, Trade and the Community," speech by Member of the European Parliament Gijs de Vries, Centre for European Policy Studies, Brussels, June 20, 1987.
12. *A Letter from Europe*, Delegation of the European Communities, January 25, 1988.
13. "Commission Vows to Uphold Free Movement of Workers," *Europe*, May 1988, p. 44.

14. "Completion of the internal market: approximation of indirect tax rates and harmonization of indirect tax structure," Global Communication from the Commission, COM(87) 320, August 26, 1987, p. 7.

15. Ibid.

16. "Rocard joins UK in opposition to Commission tax proposals," *Financial Times,* September 12, 1988.

17. "The quest for tax harmony," *Financial Times,* August 22, 1988; and "The smug debtor," *The Economist,* September 3, 1988, p. 70.

18. "Lawson attacks Brussels' plans to standardise VAT," *Financial Times,* April 9, 1988.

19. *Fiscal Harmonisation: An Analysis of the European Commission's Proposals* (London: Institute for Fiscal Studies, 1988).

20. "Green Paper on copyright and the challenge of technology—copyright issues requiring immediate action," COM(88) 172, June 7, 1988.

21. COM(85) 310, paragraph 72.

22. "Commission Programme for 1988" (Brussels: Commission of the European Communities, 1988).

23. "The Social Dimension of the Internal Market," *Social Europe* (Luxembourg: Commission of the European Communities, 1988).

24. "Conclusions of the European Council," Hanover, June 27–28, 1988.

25. "Social Dimension of the Internal Market," SEC(88) 1148, September 14, 1988.

26. "Europe 1992" (London and Dublin: Industry and Services Union, August 1988), pp. 9 and 11.

27. "EC faces up to merger worries as 1992 beckons," *Financial Times,* March 3, 1988.

28. "Brussels orders repayment of Ecu 747m in state aid," *Financial Times,* June 3, 1988.

29. Jacques Pelkmans, "A Grand Design by the Piece?" in *1992: One European Market?* (Florence: European University Institute, 1988), p. 386.

30. COM(85) 310, paragraph 95.

31. "Proposal for a Second Council Directive on the coordination of laws, regulations and administrative provisions relating to the taking-up and pursuit of the business of credit institutions and amending Directive 77/780/EEC," COM(87) 715, February 16, 1988. See also George S. Zavvos, "1992: One Market," *International Financial Law Review,* March 1988, pp. 7–11.

32. Pelkmans and Winters, *Europe's Domestic Market,* p. 51.

33. "Proposal for a Council Directive on the coordination of certain provisions laid down by law, regulation or administrative action in Member States concerning the pursuit of broadcasting activities," COM(86) 146, June 6, 1986.

34. COM(85) 310, paragraph 81.

35. "Brussels tries again to take public procurement tendering across borders," *Financial Times,* June 27, 1988.

How a Single Market Will Change the Community

5

It is axiomatic that completion of the internal market will result in a strikingly different Community—a more powerful, more efficient economic unit better able to meet competition in the EC and on world markets. Indeed, largely because of the increasingly accepted belief that the many obstacles to an integrated market were levying a heavy economic cost on the Community, the EC launched its drive toward an integrated market. That view was well reflected in the White Paper's assertion that "completion of the Internal Market will provide an indispensable base for increasing the prosperity of the Community as a whole."[1] However, curiously enough, no extensive analysis of the consequences of taking such action had been made. Prior to 1985, there had been only general assessments or partial or anecdotal estimates of the costs of a fragmented Community, as in the Albert-Ball report that described, for example, the cost of paperwork and delays for road transportation at the internal borders and the total bill for the EC's highly protected public procurement sector.[2]

RESULTS OF CURRENT ANALYSES

It was only once the process was under way that the Commission decided it would be necessary, for political as well as economic reasons, to assess the consequences of successful completion of the program. Accordingly, in 1986 the Commission began such a study. Interestingly, the study was couched in terms of the costs of "non-Europe"—in other words, the costs to the Community of *not* completing the internal market. Leadership for the task was entrusted to Paolo Cecchini, a recently retired Deputy Director General, who had been responsible for the internal market. The project turned into a large-scale undertaking, involving 200 people and costing about $5 million. It also took considerably longer than planned, coming out about a year behind schedule in May 1988.

It is the only comprehensive analysis available of the impact of completing the internal market. The Cecchini report consists of a 125-page overview of the analysis and conclusions,[3] a longer study of the potential micro- and macroeconomic impacts, summaries of the many individual studies in specific manufacturing and service sectors, and a survey of attitudes and expectations of industrial company managers. Finally, for those wishing the ultimate in detail, the Commission has published the complete sectoral studies—about 6,000 pages that include information on the activities of 11,000 firms.

The Cecchini report analyzes the effects of completing the internal market on two types of cost: those that will be immediately reduced by the elimination of barriers and the much greater costs resulting from economic inefficiencies that will be replaced by more dynamic practices over time. It foresees the development of a self-sustaining circle of events, starting with the removal of barriers, which leads to a supply-side shock to the economy, then to lower costs and prices, and finally to greater competition. The four main consequences will be a reduction of costs, improved efficiency, new patterns of competition, and increased innovation.

Based on extensive macroeconomic and microeconomic analysis, the report compares maintenance of the status quo with the situation that would obtain, at an indeterminate date, upon completion of the internal market; it looks at the immediate effects and the longer-term (and more significant) consequences. In doing so, it assesses the results expected from removal of the barriers and from adoption of the "accompanying economic policy measures," defined as policies that recognize the potential for faster growth, such as increased public investment and reductions in income tax. The conclusions of the Cecchini report (offered with a 30 percent margin of error) are that completion of the internal market will result in far-reaching gains for the EC—an increase in the Community's GDP by between 4.5 percent and 7 percent, an increase in employment by between 2 million and 5 million, a lowering of consumer prices in the range of 4.5 percent to 6 percent, a decrease in the public budgetary deficit by up to 2 percent of GDP, and an improvement in the Community's external balance by up to 1 percent of GDP.[4]

However, the report and Commission leaders have emphasized that the operative word is "potential"; as Commission President Delors put it, the figures represent a "potential which has to be used by the governments of the member states, industry and the other economic participants."[5] Similarly, in his forward to the report, Lord Cockfield spoke of the "great opportunities" that completion of the internal market will open up for growth, job creation, economies of scale, improved productivity and profitability, healthier competition, professional and business mobility, stable prices, and consumer choice.[6] The report presupposes that these opportunities will be seized—the private sector making the necessary changes in business strategy and governments ensuring the full adoption of the White Paper measures on schedule.

The only other economic analysis of the effects of completion of the internal market was undertaken by Data Resources Inc. in 1987.[7] However, because the DRI study was produced for its clients, it has not been published, and only a few highlights have been made available to the public. DRI's conclusions are far less favorable than those of the Cecchini report. The study forecasts an increase of about one-half a percentage point in the Community's GDP by 1992 and a modest gain in employment of about 300,000 people by 1995, though in the longer run it expects stronger gains in demand, output and employment. At the same time, DRI anticipates a greater impact at the disaggregated industrial level, such as an increased consumption of consumer durables (for example, cars and consumer electronics) in the major EC industrial countries, along with many instances of increased import penetration. However, it is by no means clear that the DRI and Cecchini studies are comparable; they appear to differ significantly in their approach and methodology. In any event, because only sparse information is available on the DRI study, caution should be exercised in comparing the two reports.

A noteworthy study was also issued by the Royal Institute of International Affairs in London in April 1988.[8] This report is not an economic analysis, but rather focuses on the objectives and benefits of an integrated market, the White Paper's strategy and its adequacy for achieving the objectives, and other measures and conditions that will be required to make the EC's economy more dynamic. The authors (one British, one Dutch) believe that "the White Paper proposals are at best a necessary, but not a sufficient, condition of achieving an irreversibly unified market by 1993."[9] According to the study, the full potential of the integrated market can be best exploited if the Community undertakes a vigorous competition policy, maintains an externally open market, follows predictably stable macroeconomic policies, and adopts appropriate coordinated policies on research and development, legal rules and regional policy to correct or prevent "market failure." The potential obstacles to success identified by the study are the less-than-favorable medium-term economic outlook, problems of adjustment that may cause domestic pressures to slow or halt progress on the integration process, pitfalls in the decisionmaking and bargaining processes, and uncertainty as to whether the necessary budgetary resources for structural adjustment in the less developed areas will be available. In conclusion, the study lists three possible outcomes—an "economically thorough" internal market; the removal of barriers to market access but little progress elsewhere (e.g., financial services, public procurement, and state aids); and an unsatisfactory "Europe a la carte"—but it makes no predictions.

CHANGING PATTERNS OF COMPETITION, REGIONAL DISPARITY AND CROSS-BORDER ACTIVITY

Based on the analyses described above, generally accepted economic theory and actions taking place in the EC private sector, one can predict with confidence that as the impediments to conducting business across member state borders are removed, significant economic benefits will accrue in the Community. These should take the form of lower production costs and the advantages of economies of scale and should ultimately result in lower prices and increased demand—hence benefits to both producers and consumers. The net effect, it must be emphasized, will be to sharpen competition significantly in manufacturing and services inside the EC—among EC and non-EC firms operating inside the Common Market—and, no less important, by EC firms operating outside the EC, whether in the United States or in third country markets.

The effects of completion of the internal market will by no means be uniform among sectors of the economy, types of firms, member countries, or even regions. The changes that will take place will result from numerous individual decisions by individual participants in the economic life of the Community, taken in response to the market-opening measures of the 1992 program. For that reason as well, more uncertainty necessarily surrounds the outcome when more than a macroeconomic analysis is undertaken.

An important issue in this regard is the implications for regional policy in the Community. The economic disparities among the member states are considerable: per capita GDP ranges from $15,000 in Denmark and $13,000-$14,000 in France and Germany to $6,000 in Ireland and Spain, $4,000 in Greece and under $3,000 in Portugal.[10] More than 20 percent of the EC's population live in areas where per capita income is 80 percent or less of the Community's average.[11] Under these circumstances, fears have been expressed that this regional "imbalance" will be aggravated by completion of the internal market program.

In response to these concerns, a section was included in the Single European Act on "economic and social cohesion," which stipulated that the Community "shall aim at reducing disparities between various regions and the backwardness of the least-favoured regions."[12] Reflecting that spirit, the European Council agreed to a doubling of structural development funds for the regions in early 1988 (discussed in Chapter 4). While questions have been raised about the absorptive capacity of these areas and, on the other hand, about the adequacy of these funds, a more intriguing—and at the moment unanswerable—question is what will be the relative gains and losses for the less developed (largely southern) regions. To what extent will they benefit from the inflow of capital attracted by lower labor and other costs; to what extent will they lose business to other regions? To what extent will the EC be willing to ease the burden of transition by such actions as public procurement preference and derogations from EC regulations?

The effect of the market integration process on enterprises will obviously depend on many variables. At a minimum, the process will entail dislocations. There will be losers as well as gainers among the various economic and social groups, and undoubtedly not only in the short term. Unemployment will necessarily rise in certain areas, whether or not offset by employment increases elsewhere, with attendant social and political pressures. The extent to which enterprises seek to relocate, amalgamate and/or expand their operations will depend on many factors. These include the extent of fixed investment in existing facilities, the availability of skilled workers, inducements offered by potential new locations, the conditions dictated by local law and practice on plant closings and layoffs, the trade-off between economies of scale and proximity to sources and suppliers, and, of course, the extent to which enterprises will respond to new opportunities. Finally, there are uncertainties as to the effect of the internal market program on small and medium sized enterprises. While some observers have expressed concern that these will be at greater risk, others believe they can benefit from new niche markets. In any event, the Commission is providing informational and other program assistance to these firms.[13]

In assessing the changes that will take place in the Community, account must be taken of the range of restrictions and structural rigidities that presently exist in the EC economy. Many of these are not directly affected by the measures in the White Paper, and yet they are important determinants of economic efficiency and developments in the Community. Examples range from government-regulated store hours and restrictions on hiring and firing workers to distortions of competition resulting from nationalized industries and government monopolies. Although it is hazardous to generalize, it can be expected that many of these restrictions and rigidities will resist the pressures of change arising from completion of the internal market, thus slowing the process of economic integration.

As discussed in Chapter 4, the private sector in the Community is actively reviewing the implications for it of the program to complete the internal market. Widespread anecdotal evidence shows that not only is the level of awareness of the program's content increasing, but that more and more companies are assessing their strategies with a view to maximizing their position in the expected integrated market. For many, this has meant seeking to establish, or expand, an EC dimension. Indeed, the level of cross-border activity among EC firms has increased enormously since "1992" loomed on the horizon.

Mergers have risen sharply in the Community: foreign takeovers increased by 50 percent in Germany in 1987;[14] in the same year, cross-border bids from France, Germany and the United Kingdom were more than double the 1983–85 average;[15] and inter-EC mergers increased 45 percent in 1986–87.[16] Obviously, this activity was not solely motivated by firms' desire to expand into an integrated EC market. For many companies, it represented a response to the opportunities and dangers of the increased globalization taking place in the world economy; for others, it represented an effort to strengthen a domestic industry against outside competition (e.g., French insurance and Spanish banks); and for some, it represented a certain element of panic. This activity is by no means limited to EC companies. The pace of Japanese investment has increased appreciably, and a number of major moves have been taken by companies in European countries that are not members of the EC. The most spectacular of these was the merger between Brown Boveri (Swiss) and ASEA (Swedish) to form the world's largest electrical engineering group, a merger clearly entered into with the integrated EC market in mind.

Not only is the pace of mergers increasing, but so are hostile takeovers, a new phenomenon for many countries; the most spectacular of these was the attempt in early 1988 by Italian entrepreneur Carlo De Benedetti to gain control of Societe Generale de Belgique. But cross-border activity covers many more forms than mergers and acquisitions; also involved are joint ventures, interlocking shareholding and other forms of asset exchanges, all of which are being examined and used as enterprises move farther beyond national borders.

MOVEMENT TOWARD MONETARY COOPERATION

While monetary policy issues were consciously excluded from the White Paper (discussed in Chapter 3), increasing support has been given to the view that a natural, and even necessary, consequence of completion of the internal market will be a progression of moves: first, the "strengthening" of the EMS, which mainly means participation by the United Kingdom in the EMS exchange rate mechanism to form an effective EC-wide exchange rate system; next, the establishment of a common currency, most likely through increasing acceptance and use of the ECU, a process that is still in its infancy; and, finally, the creation of an EC central bank. Influential in propagating this view was a 1987 report written for the Commission to examine the consequences of the accession of Portugal and Spain to the Community and of the EC's program to complete the internal market.[17] The study concluded that stronger EMS mechanisms and strengthened monetary policy coordination were required; however, it also noted the eventual Community objective of monetary union, which would require a single currency and a central bank.

Until recently the latter was a taboo subject. However, in recent months it has generated a remarkable degree of public debate and considerable support. After the idea of an EC central bank was floated in late 1987 by the French Finance Minister, it was endorsed by the German government, and the subject was placed on the agenda of the European Council in June 1988. At that meeting, a high-level study group was established under Commission President Delors to examine over the following 12 months possible improvements in European monetary cooperation. Although no specific mention was made in the Council's communiqué of a single currency or central bank, in deference to U.K. opposition to the consideration of any proposals involving a diminution of national sovereignty over monetary matters, the group will necessarily study these two issues.

It should be emphasized that movement down this path will be slow and tentative; it is most improbable that any concrete actions on a central bank will be taken before the main elements of the internal market have been completed, although there could well be somewhat greater coordination of monetary policy and increased use of the ECU for international transactions and accounts. Apart from national sovereignty—of concern not solely to the United Kingdom—a number of basic issues will need to be addressed by the member states. Fundamental is whether an EC central bank should follow the German model of an independent institution committed to maintaining price stability—in essence, an extension of the Bundesbank (and the Deutschemark) to an EC basis—with its tight monetary policy, low interest rates and low growth, or whether it should involve greater control by national governments with more expansionist objectives. While such a system appeals to some elements in the Community, it implies far-reaching changes in economic policy in a number of member countries. Despite the very difficult decisions that would have to be taken, the process toward an integrated market, with free movement of trade and capital, will in all probability move the Community toward a comprehensive EMS (including full British participation) as well as a single currency and some form of centralized banking.

POLITICAL IMPLICATIONS

Although this study addresses economic and not political issues, the political implications of the program to complete the
internal market cannot be ignored. While the early champions of
European unification envisaged political as well as economic union, the greatest progress has occurred on the economic side.
However, an important political step was taken when the Single
European Act formalized the system that had developed of consultation and coordination among the member states on foreign
policy issues. Beyond that, the development of the integrated
market will likely provide an important impetus to increased political cooperation in two ways. First, it will require the member
states to discuss and decide on issues not strictly or exclusively
economic in nature, such as immigration and drug trafficking, that
often involve politicians and government officials not normally
concerned with issues in a Community context. Second, as the
member states and their citizens increasingly interact across the
range of economic issues, the pattern and practice of political
interaction is bound to become more an accepted way of life.

Another aspect of the political issue is the relationship between the EC and the six nonmember European countries that
comprise the European Free Trade Association (EFTA)—Austria,
Finland, Iceland, Norway, Sweden, and Switzerland. These countries have benefited from free trade area agreements with the Community (i.e., tariff-free movement of goods to and from the EC),
as well as a number of Europe-wide activities, notably the establishment of technical standards.

With the development of the internal market program, however, the option of membership in the Community as a way of
protecting vital economic interests has become the subject of serious debate in the EFTA countries. Although each of the six
countries had previously taken a decision not to seek membership—in the case of Austria, Sweden and Switzerland because of
their policy of political neutrality—the perceived danger from remaining outside a truly integrated EC is causing careful rethink-
ing (see Chapter 9). The most likely applicants appear to be Norway, which opted against membership in a close vote in 1972,
and Austria, possibly with the blessings of the Soviet Union, one
of the guarantors of Austrian neutrality. The economic concerns
are at least as weighty in Sweden and Switzerland, but the political obstacles to membership are greater. In any event, no move
toward membership will be given serious consideration by the EC
in the near future. In addition to the fact that this would require
the EC to deal with the possible conflict between its unification
goals and EFTA neutrality (except for Norway), the Community

would have to divert its attention to application negotiations while pressing forward to complete the internal market. Thus, at least in the short term, the EFTA countries will have to face the challenges of "1992" as outsiders.

The other significant political relationship between the Community and a neighboring country is that with the German Democratic Republic. During the negotiations on formation of the EC, the Federal Republic of Germany insisted on inclusion of a protocol that recognized trade between the two Germanies as constituting internal trade. Thus, an export from the GDR to the Federal Republic is not subject to tariffs or other import restrictions, whereas a GDR good entering another EC member state (directly or through the Federal Republic) is classified as an import into the EC and treated accordingly. The potential significance of this partial free trade agreement on an integrated EC market is unclear; although the risk has always existed, it could increase the possibility of "leakage" of goods into the EC, whether from Eastern Europe or elsewhere.

NOTES

1. COM(85) 310, paragraph 21.
2. Michel Albert and James Ball, *Towards European Recovery in the 1980s: Report to the European Parliament* (New York: Praeger Special Studies, 1984).
3. Paolo Cecchini, *The European Challenge 1992* (Wildwood House, Aldershot [U.K.], 1988).
4. Ibid., pp. 93–97. The macroeconomic gains projected are: + 4.5% GDP, - 6.1% prices, + 2.2% of GDP in public finance balance, + 1% of GDP in external balance, + 1.8 million jobs (i.e., about - 1.5% unemployment rate). However, if these are accompanied by appropriate macroeconomic policies (increase in public investment, increased tax reductions, and so forth), these figures would become + 7% GDP, - 4.5% prices, + 0.4% public finance balance, - 0.2% external balance, + 5 million jobs. Also of interest is the breakdown of some of the medium-term estimates: (a) removal of border controls: + 0.33% GDP, + 1% prices, + 0.2% public finance balance; (b) opening of public procurement: + 0.5% GDP, - 1.4% prices, + 0.3% public finance balance, + 0.1% external balance, + 400,000 jobs; (c) liberalization of financial services: + 1.5% GDP, - 1.4% prices, + 500,000 jobs; (d) supply-side effects on business: + 2% GDP, - 2% prices, + 0.6% public finance balance, + 2.4% external balance. For a more detailed analysis, see also Alasdair Smith and Anthony Venables, *Completing the Internal Market in the European Community: Some Industry Simulations*, Discussion Paper No. 233 (London, Centre for Economic Policy Research, March 1988).
5. "Gilded vision of 1992 for the Community," *Financial Times*, March 30, 1988.
6. Cecchini, *European Challenge*, p. xiii.
7. "The European Internal Market," executive summary (Brussels: Data Resources Inc., 1987).
8. Jacques Pelkmans and Alan Winters, *Europe's Domestic Market*, Royal Institute of International Affairs Chatham House Papers No. 43 (London: Routledge, 1988).
9. Ibid., p. 10.
10. *Main Economic Indicators* (Paris: Organization for Economic Cooperation and Development, May 1988).

11.   "Two sides to Europe," *The Economist*, June 27, 1987, p. 71.

12.   Single European Act, Title V.

13.   See "E.C. Policy on Small and Medium-Sized Companies," *Europe*, September 1988, pp. 24–26.

14.   "When the choice is buy or be bought," *Financial Times*, May 9, 1988.

15.   Booz, Allen & Hamilton, quoted in *Business International*, June 27, 1988, p. 202.

16.   "17th Report on Competition Policy," COM(88) 232, May 26, 1988, p. 278. Data is June 1986-May 1987.

17.   Tommaso Padoa-Schioppa, *Efficiency, Stability and Equity* (Oxford: Oxford University Press, 1987).

— PART II —

The U.S. Economic Stake in the EC

6

The United States and the 12 members of the European Community are the world's two major economic blocs. Together they account for almost one-half of the world's GDP and about one-third of global trade.[1] Each is the other's most important trading partner, with bilateral trade reaching just under $150 billion in 1987. Similarly, each is the leading foreign investor in the other's territory.[2] In fact, a myriad of economic relationships has developed between the United States and the Community, mirroring the increasing economic interdependence throughout the world and covering the entire range of economic activities.

Rather than try to describe and analyze this complex relationship, it is more germane to the purpose of this study to narrow the focus to the activities of U.S. firms inside the Community—that is, U.S. exports to the EC and U.S. direct investment there. These two aspects of the US-EC economic relationship will be most vitally affected by developments in the Community's internal market.

First, a look at exports. In 1987, U.S. merchandise exports to the EC totaled $60.6 billion, representing 24 percent of U.S. global exports.[3] In order of magnitude, the leading export items were automatic data processing machinery and equipment, transportation equipment (largely aircraft), electrical machinery, power-generating equipment, and professional, scientific and controlling instruments. The largest increases have taken place in the first two categories, but all have registered significant gains[4] (see Appendix A).

A brief historical review reveals the continuing, and for the most part increasing, importance of the EC as a market for U.S. goods (see Appendix B). For example, U.S. exports to the EC of $4 billion in 1960, the early days of the Community, accounted for 20 percent of total U.S. exports; this figure rose to $8 billion (19 percent of the total) in 1970, climbed to $54 billion (24 percent) in 1980, and maintained that share in 1987.[5] These figures pertain to the membership of the Community as it existed at the time—in other words, the original 6 countries expanded to 9 in 1973, to 10 in 1981 and to the current 12 in 1986. Although the accession of the United Kingdom in 1973 skews the figures in a sense, a comparison of historical data for the EC's present membership would be less relevant because such statistics would not reflect the growing size and economic importance of the Community as its membership has expanded.

The above U.S. government statistics cover exports of goods, but not exports of services, which have grown in importance by all accounts. Despite the increased attention being paid to this sector, no generally accepted system of measuring service exports has been developed. The only official statistics available, compiled by the U.S. Department of Commerce, indicate $17.5 billion of service exports to the EC in 1987, or 29 percent of total U.S. exports.[6] According to these statistics, service exports have sharply increased over the past two decades, up from $900 million (14 percent of the total) in 1966 (see Appendix C). However, it is generally accepted that the official data understate, perhaps by as much as one-half, the actual value of such exports.[7]

The other important aspect of the relationship is the U.S. physical presence inside the Community. In 1987, U.S. direct investment in the EC was $122 billion, accounting for 40 percent of total U.S. foreign investment.[8] Of this total, more than one-half, $70 billion, was in manufacturing, with $19 billion accounted for by petroleum, $17 billion by banking and other financial sectors, and $11 billion by wholesale trade. Although these figures are based on book value and thus understate actual market value, they nonetheless represent a useful benchmark. In terms of the historical record, U.S. investment in the EC (as it was constituted at the time) was $2.6 billion (8 percent of the total) in 1960, rose to $11.5 billion (15 percent) in 1970, and then jumped to $77.2 billion (36 percent) in 1980 (about one-half the leap that occurred during the 1970s was accounted for by the U.K.'s accession); see Appendix D.

Of course, the investment aggregates do not tell the full story. In many areas—geographically and sectorally—the U.S. presence is quite significant in terms of employment, output, income, and tax revenue. Sales by U.S. manufacturing subsidiaries in the EC are estimated to have ranged between $350 billion and $430 billion annually over the past five years (with the higher figure being the most recent estimate).[9] Although it is more difficult to measure adequately U.S. activities in the service sector than in manufacturing, they are nevertheless of sizable proportion.

One final consideration is in order. It would be erroneous to think of U.S. economic interests as neatly divided into the two categories of exporters and investors. In fact, a significant volume of export is conducted by U.S. parent firms to their subsidiaries, and this appears to have increased in rough proportion to U.S. investments in the EC. Based on information provided by U.S. firms completing questionnaires on investment for the U.S. government, $18 billion of $53 billion of total U.S. exports to the EC in 1986 were accounted for by exports to U.S. subsidiaries.[10] Regardless of how precise this calculation is, the volume of such export is undoubtedly significant. According to anecdotal evidence from several U.S. firms with large investments in the EC, a considerable share of the exports from their U.S. operations goes to their subsidiaries—in some cases as much as 90 percent—and a relevant proportion of output from their operations in the EC is sourced from the United States—in the 10 to 20 percent and above range.

These figures demonstrate the critical stake the United States has in the European Community. Thus, changes within the Community are bound to impinge on the interests of U.S. participants in that market.

NOTES

1. GDP data for 1986 are derived from Central Intelligence Agency, *Handbook of Economic Statistics* (Washington, 1987), p. 4; trade data for 1987 are derived from International Monetary Fund, *International Financial Statistics* (Washington, July 1988), and from Statistical Office of the European Communities, *Eurostat* (Luxembourg, 1988).

2. U.S. Department of Commerce, *1987 U.S. Foreign Trade Highlights* (Washington, 1988); Commerce Department, *Survey of Current Business* (June 1988); and *Eurostat* (1988).

3. *1987 U.S. Foreign Trade Highlights* (1988).

4. This ranking is based on two-digit SITC codes from unpublished data of the Commerce Department.

5. For sources, see Appendix B.

6. *Survey of Current Business* (June 1988), pp. 41 and 60.

7. Congress of the United States, Office of Technology Assessment, *Trade in Services: Exports and Foreign Revenues* (Washington, 1986), p. 3.

8. Data for 1987 are contained in *Survey of Current Business* (June 1988), p. 81. For sources of historical data, see Appendix D.

9. Unpublished Commerce Department data.

10. Unpublished Commerce Department data.

Implications of the Integrated Market for U.S. Business

7

Completion of the internal market will present U.S. business an essentially barrier-free market in place of what had largely been 12 separate entities. Consequently, there will be not only opportunities but also incentives for firms to expand their geographic coverage to serve a larger customer base with greater facility. Equally important, this will apply to all firms, whether they are headquartered or operate inside the Community and whether they are U.S., EC or third country firms.

With the changes that will result from the integrated market, it is relevant to ask whether U.S. firms can expect to gain at the expense of their EC and other competitors. It is widely asserted in the EC that foreign—in particular U.S.—multinationals have been the major beneficiaries of the opportunities presented by the EC's formation and development. This has resulted from their global approach to markets and their experience operating in and among foreign countries, as opposed to a greater tendency by Community firms to maintain a base in their home country and satellite operations in other member countries. As one observer put it, U.S. multinationals believed there was a Common Market before it existed. Of course, that analysis is an oversimplification of a dynamic process, particularly as EC firms have expanded their activities both inside and outside the Community.

One effect of an integrated EC market will be to facilitate the operation of EC firms across member state borders; at the same time, this market could reduce advantages enjoyed by some U.S. multinationals from the fragmented markets of the EC. Indeed, it has been suggested that the "star performers" of the integrated Common Market could well be the EC mavericks, who have nothing to lose by challenging the traditional order.[1] On the other hand, to the extent that U.S. multinationals have developed strong positions in the EC, they could build on their experience and expertise to further the advantages already gained. In any event, there is little basis on which to generalize as to the likely relative gains of domestic and foreign companies.

It is clear, however (see Chapter 5), that completion of the internal market will vastly enhance the potential competitive position of EC firms not only inside the Community but also in other markets, including the United States. Accordingly, account will have to be taken of the effects this will have on the global competitive situation—a set of issues beyond the scope of this study.

IMPORTANCE OF VARIOUS BARRIERS

In assessing the implications of an integrated market for U.S. business, a distinction should be made on the basis of the degree of consequence to U.S. firms of elimination of the barriers addressed in the White Paper.

Lesser direct benefits will accrue to U.S. firms by elimination of the following barriers:

(1) *Border controls.* Cost savings will, of course, result from the elimination of formalities and delays in connection with the physical movement of goods across national frontiers, thus benefiting any firms involved in transporting goods across EC borders. However, this does not appear to have been a major obstacle for U.S. firms.

(2) *Freedom of movement and right of establishment of people.* Although there will be some benefits to firms using the services of such professionals, and potentially considerable benefits to those engaged in these occupations, the obstacles and costs appear to have been marginal for U.S. firms.

(3) *Indirect tax harmonization.* The different systems and rates do not appear to have impinged significantly on the operation of U.S. firms since the competitive distortions are minimal. U.S. firms' concerns have been directed more toward the differences among the direct tax systems.

An intermediate category of barriers of *moderate interest* to U.S. firms consists of:

(1) *Common legal framework.* To the extent that Community actions standardize and simplify procedures among the member countries, this will reduce costs and the physical burden of having to deal with different legal regimes in cross-border operations. However, U.S. firms have not considered these unduly onerous, for the most part. On the other hand, the key factor for U.S. companies will be the nature of whatever measures are adopted. EC-wide measures could result in savings in time and expense and/or could introduce disadvantageous elements (as in the case of social policy). One particular area of interest to U.S. firms will be intellectual property.

(2) *Capital liberalization.* At present, U.S. firms face few major problems in the EC relating to raising capital, moving it or generally conducting financial transactions. However, liberalizing capital movements throughout the Community is a crucial precondition to deregulating the financial service sector, and in this area U.S. interests are significant.

U.S. interests will be *vitally affected* in the following areas:

(1) *Regulation of services.* The terms and conditions under which U.S. providers of services will be able to operate inside the Community will be critical. U.S. firms active in areas such as financial services and information technology, both key sectors in industrial societies, have been at the forefront in developing new products and techniques. Although U.S. firms are well represented in the EC service sector, it will be essential for them to have maximum opportunity to participate in a rapidly changing environment.

(2) *Regulations and standards.* The outcome of the various efforts in the EC to harmonize regulations and standards will have major implications for the ability of U.S. firms to compete in the Community. This is particularly, but by no means solely, the case in the high technology area. The key consideration is whether the process will result in or be used to establish regulations and standards of an exclusionary nature, which will make it more difficult for U.S. products to enter or circulate in the EC. That will be as much a question of testing and certification procedures as the method of establishment and content of regulations and standards.

(3) *Public procurement.* Opening up the vast EC public procurement market will provide wide opportunities for U.S. business, particularly in fields such as telecommunications, information technology and power equipment where the United States is competitive. Of particular relevance for U.S. firms will be the conditions established for eligibility to bid.

IMPLICATIONS FOR U.S. EXPORTERS

Two critical considerations underlie the implications for actual and potential U.S. exporters to the EC with completion of the internal market.

- There will be greater opportunities arising from economic growth, but these will be tempered by significantly greater competition inside the Community.
- There will be little change in the level of protection at the EC external border; however, the measures that affect exporters will take place inside the EC.

An integrated EC market will almost certainly result in a higher level of economic activity—and thus a higher level of demand and consumption—than otherwise. That obviously implies greater opportunities for products exported to the Community.

However, it is difficult, if not impossible, to forecast the extent to which this increased demand will be satisfied by imported rather than domestic goods. Not only is the debate unresolved over whether customs unions (or more far-reaching economic integration, as would be the case with the EC) generate or divert trade, but the outcome also depends on many imponderables, of which the future course of exchange rates is the most prominent. Suffice it to say that the forces freed by the market-opening measures of the White Paper will increase the intensity of competition for these larger markets.

In considering the potential for the Community to adopt policies affecting U.S. exports to the EC, it is appropriate to begin with the EC's *common external tariff*. The establishment of tariff rates is governed by the provisions of the General Agreement on Tariffs and Trade. Under the GATT, it would not be possible for the EC to assert that completion of the internal market produced benefits to third countries that justified increasing tariffs. Such action could only be taken if accompanied by offsetting compensatory reductions in trade barriers, and that would obviously negate the purpose of raising tariffs in the first place. In any event, there are no indications that the EC contemplates any changes in tariff levels.

However, one area directly affecting imports that the EC will have to address in connection with completion of the internal market is *import quotas*. At present, individual member states maintain as many as 1,000 individual quotas or other measures restricting imports (including the increasingly prevalent "voluntary" export restraint agreements and industry-to-industry agreements).[2] Most of these are country-specific, largely aimed at imports from Japan and the newly industrializing Asian countries as well as the nonmarket countries of Eastern Europe. Apart from some restrictions imposed by Portugal and Spain, most of which are scheduled to be phased out by 1992, the EC quotas and related measures will have little, if any, impact on U.S. exports.

Although these restrictions are sanctioned by the Treaty of Rome, they are inconsistent with an integrated market because they represent differing trade policies of the member states and require border controls. Other than maintaining the status quo—which would impede establishment of a single market—the two alternatives for the Community are to phase out these arrangements entirely or to transform them into EC-wide quotas. Clearly, neither will be easy for the Community, either in terms of satisfying conflicting interests among the member states or of fulfilling its obligations to its trading partners.

The two most significant sets of quotas are those on textiles and automobiles. Negotiated by the EC under the terms of the

Multi-Fiber Agreement, textile quotas have been established for the Community and/or individual member states. None applies to exports from the United States. It is expected that these quotas will eventually be phased into Community restrictions applying exclusively to the EC, even though in some cases that would imply a higher level of protection.

Probably more difficult to deal with will be the quotas and other forms of restrictions imposed by several member states on Japanese automobile imports. These range from informal limitations in the United Kingdom of about 11 percent to a ceiling of 3 percent in the French market and 3,000 vehicles in Italy. The extension of quotas from a national basis (but only in certain member states) to a comprehensive EC-wide basis would presumably represent an overall increase in the level of protection, and certainly would do so in member states not presently restricting such imports. Not surprisingly, EC automobile manufacturers have vigorously argued in favor of maintaining restrictions on Japanese imports. One proposal has been to tie the level of Japanese imports to EC penetration of the Japanese automobile market. For example, the European car manufacturers association has suggested freezing Japanese imports at the existing level of 10 percent of the EC market until EC manufacturers reach half that level of the Japanese market (compared to 3 percent at present).[3]

Whatever the form, it is highly unlikely that the EC will unilaterally phase out its restrictions on Japanese automobile imports. Not only would the adjustment for countries such as France and Italy be enormous, but that action would run directly counter to the EC's prevailing, and strongly supported, "get tough" policy with Japan. It is far more likely that the Community will use the existence of the restrictions as leverage in seeking to improve its access in the Japanese market.

U.S. interests are potentially at stake in connection with this issue because of the Japanese investment in automobile manufacture in the United States. It is by no means improbable that the Japanese automobile manufacturers will choose—perhaps even in the near future—to export automobiles manufactured in the United States to the EC, as they have begun to do in the case of some Asian markets, including Japan. At that time, questions may well be raised in the EC as to whether such vehicles fall under the import restrictions on Japanese automobiles. At issue would be the "origin" of these automobiles—whether they should be classified as American or Japanese. The general rule in the EC is that the "origin" of a product is determined by the location of the "last substantial transformation," which would clearly appear to be the United States. Nonetheless, depending on the circumstances, it is conceivable that the EC would decide to consider these vehicles as Japanese for quota purposes. The same principle could also be applied to U.S. automobiles with a high Japanese (or at least non-U.S.) content, as it could to U.S. exports of other products from Japanese investment subject to import restrictions by the EC as "Japanese products" (see Chapter 9).

Another area where EC action could reduce access for U.S. exports is *antidumping* policies—in other words, by imposing more stringent rules against goods deemed to be imported at less than fair value. In the past few years, the EC has clearly tightened up its procedures in areas such as assembly of products from imported components, services and absorption of costs of dumping duties. In particular, it has adopted a very firm posture in dealing with antidumping cases involving Japanese, and more recently Korean, exporters. Although most unlikely, circumstances could develop in which U.S. firms find themselves subject to a similar attitude.

IMPLICATIONS FOR U.S. INVESTORS

As in the case of exporters, present and potential U.S. investors in the Community must recognize that an integrated EC market will be larger, more dynamic and more competitive. Thus, it will present new opportunities as well as risks.

The first, and in many ways basic, question to be asked regarding investment activities of U.S. firms in the EC is whether they are accorded *national treatment*—whether they receive treatment no less favorable in like circumstances than that accorded domestic firms. Up to now, the question has been posed essentially in terms of treatment by member states, whereas in the future it will be posed increasingly on a Community basis. The principle of national treatment reflects the common interests of the world's industrialized nations, all with significant foreign investments. For that reason, members of the Organization for Economic Cooperation and Development (OECD), which includes the United States and the EC member states, drew up the National Treatment Instrument in 1976 (a hortatory, nonbinding understanding), to which all members subscribe.

EC states have largely granted national treatment to U.S. subsidiaries. Indeed, the issue of what constitutes a "local" firm and a "foreign" firm for the most part has not arisen. However, the distinction has been made where national governments screen proposed foreign investments and in areas involving government expenditures: public procurement, assistance to industry and research and development. U.S. subsidiaries have been among the recipients of such expenditures by member governments. In public procurement, for example, U.S. firms have benefited from government contracts, both directly and as subcontractors or subsuppliers. However, with varying degrees of openness, some public entities in member states have given preference to "national" firms over "nonnational" companies: in some cases, the bid specifications are tailored to fit the requirements of a "national champion"; in others, there simply is a closed bidding procedure; alternatively, other bids may be entertained only if there is no "national champion." Another practice that on occasion has had discriminatory effects against U.S. firms is state assistance to the development or support of certain local industries. Finally, it should be noted that various restrictions exist in member states on the operations of nonnational firms in certain areas, such as financial services, telecommunications and transportation—in some cases not dissimilar from restrictions imposed in many non-EC countries, including the United States.

Turning to EC, as opposed to member state, policies regarding the treatment of foreign investment, the point of departure must be the Treaty of Rome, which clearly states that firms duly established in one of the member states shall "be treated in the same way as . . . nationals of member states."[4] Thus, the "law of the Community" makes no distinction among firms established within the Community on the basis of origin of capital or, for that matter, of size or type of investment. On that basis, one might assume that whatever changes take place within the EC as a result of the program to complete the internal market will affect all EC firms—those of "domestic origin" and those representing foreign capital—in the same manner. In other words, the advantages and opportunities will be available to both categories of enterprise in equal measure.

However, the situation is by no means as clear-cut as that. Most important, the Commission has never defined an "EC" firm, and that failure has left many questions open—even though it is not clear that there has been any specific reason or occasion to do so. This has presumably been intentional because of the apparent conflict between a literal reading of the Treaty (which implies a straightforward, no exceptions definition) and a degree of flexibility that the Commission would most likely wish to introduce. The ambiguity of approach is related to areas such as public procurement (prospectively) and research and development (actually), where the Commission, reflecting a general consensus in the EC, has been inclined to make a distinction between "EC" and "non-EC" firms.

With respect to public procurement, there is a strong disinclination in the EC to provide access to foreign firms incorporated in the Community but producing outside. In fact, the argument seems to be gaining acceptance that the origin of the goods in question should be the governing factor, not the place of incorporation. In the words of a French private sector leader, "it would be hyperliberal and idiotic to grant full access on public procurement to all firms established in the EC unless the goods were supplied from inside the Community." Similarly, a Commission official expressed the view that EC-wide public procurement should not extend to an EC-registered company consisting of a small supply office of a firm producing in Asia.

The EC has undertaken a number of Community-wide research and development programs, although they are not directly related to completion of the internal market. These R&D programs are designed to overcome some of the duplication of effort within the EC in high technology and to enhance its ability to compete in the global market. In the award of contracts under these programs, U.S. firms have been among the beneficiaries. Nevertheless, there is a pervasive belief among U.S. firms that these R&D programs are intended for "EC" firms and that the Commission, while not wanting to exclude U.S. firms as a matter of principle, tries to limit their participation to areas where they can offer some technology that would otherwise be unavailable.

It should be noted that many U.S. subsidiaries have long carried out a conscious policy of seeking to integrate into the local scene and gain acceptance as a "local" firm through means such as maintaining minimal nonnational staff, participating in local cultural and charitable activities, and downplaying U.S. origins. Although this is not possible for some firms because of their name, clear identification with the United States or sheer size, a significant number have expressed satisfaction with the degree to which they have become locally identified.

A second area requiring scrutiny in terms of investment activities of U.S. enterprises in the EC is *reciprocity*. Increasing attention is being focused in the Community on this area. The concept is straightforward: the EC should not permit nonmember firms to enjoy the benefits of an integrated market unless EC firms enjoy similar treatment in the nonmember's country. This is reflected in the White Paper. While referring to only one specific aspect of the internal market effort, the Paper states that "the commercial identity of the Community must be consolidated so that our trading partners will not be given the benefit of a wider market without themselves making similar concessions."[5] Reciprocity is also emphasized in the Cecchini report, which asserts that the EC will have the right to expect "appropriate responses" from its economic partners, notably the United States and Japan, to the "shot in the arm" given the world economy by the integrated EC economy. Calling for a "fair share-out of the burdens of global economic responsibility," the report states that market-opening measures should be "extended internationally on a firm basis of clear reciprocity."[6] But beyond these two documents, there is a growing acceptance of the concept of reciprocity in applying the market integration measures to non-EC members.

The concept has not been defined in form or scope beyond the general idea that it would provide "equivalence in . . . economic effects."[7] As interpreted by the EC, it would apply to a specific sector or industry. Reciprocity has been formally proposed, thus far, only in the directive on banking. As described in Chapter 4, under the concept of home country control, a bank of a non-EC country, duly established in an EC member state—the "home country"—would be able to operate throughout the Community under the primary supervision of that home country only if EC member institutions enjoy the same freedom of operation inside the non-EC country. This provision is aimed at Japan's restrictive policies in licensing EC banks. In addition to seeking to prevent Japanese banks from enjoying greater freedom in the EC than that accorded EC banks in Japan, the purpose is to use the desire of Japanese banks to expand into Europe as leverage to facilitate the entry of EC banks into Japan.

Irrespective of the rationale for this proposal, it has serious implications for the United States, specifically for banking but more broadly as well. It is not possible for EC banks to enjoy conditions in the United States equivalent to those proposed in the Commission's directive. Nationwide banking does not exist in the United States, and the restrictions on bank operations, whether they are through the Glass-Steagall Act or state controls, are more severe than those proposed in the directive. Although it is possible that greater flexibility in bank operations in the United States will be provided by legislation in the near future, the outcome will undoubtedly be a less liberal regime than that contemplated in the EC.

In response to U.S. concerns, some EC officials have claimed that the reciprocity provision will not cause difficulties for U.S. banks. In the first place, it is asserted, the EC recognizes that the U.S. system is different and does not wish to upset its relations with the United States; hence, it would find a pragmatic way of ensuring that U.S. banking activities in the EC were not impeded, possibly by negotiating a separate bilateral arrangement. Furthermore, it has been argued that virtually all U.S. banks that would conceivably want to be established inside the EC have done so (and, in fact, some U.S. banks have recently pulled out of Europe), making the question academic. This line of argument presupposes that the directive's reciprocity provision would not be applied retroactively to U.S. banks already established in the

Community. The wording of the proposed directive implies such is the case, but that issue has not been specifically clarified.

It is also unclear in what areas the EC may seek to introduce reciprocity beyond banking. Reciprocity has not been introduced in insurance, but it is under consideration with regard to access by third country firms to stock exchanges in the EC. On the other hand, reciprocity will not be sought in relation to merchandise trade because that would run counter to the EC's GATT obligations, which the EC has stressed it will continue to honor. Rather, reciprocity is most likely to be sought or applied by the EC in services, an area where it believes there are no applicable international rules. This could include other financial services; in addition, there is talk of inserting reciprocity into the process of opening up the EC telecommunications and public procurement markets.

To the extent that the EC bases the market-opening measures of the internal market on reciprocity, opportunities for U.S. enterprises in many areas could be put at risk. At a minimum, opportunities that otherwise would automatically become available would come into question. There undoubtedly will be some areas where the United States simply would be unable to grant reciprocal treatment, even though it does provide national treatment. For the most part, that would reflect the limits to the powers accorded the federal government under the U.S. federal system.

On a much lower level of concern, and probability, the potential exists for use of *rules of origin* against U.S. investments inside the EC. As in many other issues, EC concerns relate primarily to the Japanese, in particular the so-called screwdriver operations where investments are limited to assembly operations allegedly undertaken solely for the goods in question to be traded freely inside the EC. The EC's procedures against "screwdriver" operations were instituted specifically to prevent the establishment of firms in the EC to avoid antidumping duties. The concept could, however, be extended to other investments in the EC, whether they are U.S., Japanese or other.

In fact, there are increasing instances of member state objections to the free movement within the EC of exports from Japanese subsidiaries in other member states. This has arisen, for example, in the case of automobiles and television sets manufactured in the EC, which France has contended do not have sufficient content to justify "domestic origin" and thus to qualify for free entry as EC products. As mentioned above, the EC considers the country of origin to be that in which the "last substantial transformation" takes place; however, for some products a specific rule for determining origin has been adopted, such as a percentage of the product value or the origin of one or more particular components. To the extent that member states consider themselves threatened by production from foreign subsidiaries in other member countries, the rules of origin could be tightened to the detriment of foreign investments.

A final issue with potentially unfavorable consequences for U.S. investment in the EC is *social policy*. As described in Chapter 4, some White Paper measures under consideration contain elements of social policy such as worker participation in company management and health and safety standards, while a more general effort is being made by some in the EC to provide a greater "social dimension" to the Community's internal market program. Adoption of such measures would by definition affect the operation of firms established in the EC. Insofar as the interests of U.S. firms are concerned, the relevant issue is less that of harmonizing previously diverse laws and regulations than of the harmonized contents themselves—in particular, whether, and if so to what extent, they impede corporate decisionmaking and the cost implications.

ISSUES AFFECTING BOTH U.S. EXPORTERS AND INVESTORS

Finally, there are two key areas that will affect exporters and investors alike.

The first is *regulations and standards*. U.S. firms will benefit from a transparent system of establishing regulations and standards—open, fair and nondiscriminatory. They will also benefit from a system in which the testing and certification procedures do not limit access by non-EC firms. In assessing the present situation and prospects, however, it is important to recognize fundamental differences between the European and U.S. systems. One is that regulations and standards are generally established by governments in Europe to assure quality, whereas they are more often developed in the United States by industry and are less extensive. This difference is evident in the debate over standards for telecommunication equipment to be attached to the network, typified in the exchange between the U.S. official who asserted that the sole criterion should be whether the equipment harms the network, to which his EC counterpart responded "but what if it doesn't work?" Similarly, the EC has no tradition or system of public notice and comment on proposed regulations and standards, as practiced in the United States.

Nonetheless, there are indications that the relevant authorities in the EC are becoming more open to input from outside the Community. At least one American manufacturers association has begun a process of discussion of standards with the Commission; in another sector, the European regulatory body sent proposed regulations to U.S. suppliers for comment. More generally, many U.S. firms have indicated satisfaction with their involvement in standards setting in the EC, confirming that the extent was essentially dictated by the amount of resources they were willing to devote.

However, four caveats must be added to this optimistic picture. First, participation in standards setting is largely limited to U.S. subsidiaries in the EC, that is, firms classified as EC firms, operating either directly or through national or EC business associations. Without a direct presence in the EC, U.S. export interests will find it difficult to participate in or influence the process. In that respect, U.S. firms will be at a disadvantage compared with firms of non-EC European countries, which participate in the European standards organizations. Second, it is by no means certain that the EC authorities will recognize testing carried out in approved U.S. facilities. Although this question has not yet been considered in the EC—where the many aspects of testing and certification procedures are just coming under scrutiny (as discussed in Chapter 4)—nonacceptance of such testing would clearly put U.S. firms at a competitive disadvantage. Third, to the extent that the EC concentrates its standards efforts on Europe-wide standards in CEN and CENELEC, it reduces the resources it can devote to developing international standards in the International Organization for Standards (ISO) and the International Electrotechnical Commission (IEC), the organizations in which the United States participates.

The final and most important consideration is the regulations and standards that are ultimately established. Of critical importance to the United States is whether these are written in a manner designed to impede market access. A frequent EC argument in connection with the harmonization of regulations and standards is that the United States will be better off if it has to meet only one standard in the Community instead of as many as 12. Although undoubtedly correct in many, if not most, cases, the contents of the regulation or standard will also be relevant, particularly the extent to which it represents global standards. U.S. interests can be damaged by uniformity, as in the case of the EC-wide ban on meat from cattle fed with hormones, putting at risk all U.S. meat exports, which replaced a varied pattern in which some markets remained open to the U.S. product.

The second issue is that of access by U.S. firms to the EC *public procurement market*. While it would be ideal from a U.S. point of view for the projected opening of this market to take place on a global basis, the proposals presently under consideration would establish an EC public procurement market. This is hardly surprising because the EC has no international obligation to expand the regime beyond the Community, and in any event it will be traumatic enough for the interests involved to expand the market to the other member states. The presumption is that any EC firm will be able to compete on an equal footing for such contracts and that U.S. subsidiaries would qualify as "EC" firms. Whether they are accepted in fact as equals can only be tested by time. For firms in the United States, there are indications that the EC will consider opening at least some of its public procurement market beyond the EC, but only on the basis of reciprocal arrangements (presumably under the GATT procurement code). That could well prove difficult for the United States in view of a number of provisions that discriminate against non-U.S. suppliers, in particular, preferences given U.S. firms under various "buy America" laws at the state and federal level.

FORCES FOR—AND AGAINST—A MORE PROTECTIONIST COMMUNITY

As the EC faces decisions on the many issues described above, the key question for U.S. interests will be the nature or thrust of the Community policy toward nonmember countries. More specifically, will the EC adopt a protectionist policy, and if so to what extent? "Protectionist" is not strictly accurate because the term relates to barriers at the border, whereas the question is far broader. However, it is the handiest term and will be used here, as it is elsewhere, to denote measures designed to restrict or limit the opportunities afforded companies from nonmember countries to conduct business inside the EC.

Before examining the role of EC governments and institutions in setting policies that will affect the operations of non-EC firms, it should be noted that the program to complete the internal market was developed essentially as an EC internal matter. The issues and problems, and their solutions, were debated among the institutions, interest groups and other political, economic and social forces within the Community with little regard for their international aspects and implications. Nor were external relations dealt with in the White Paper. As one study concluded, the White Paper is not clear as to the nature and level of protection that was assumed for 1992.[8] As a Commission official explained, these issues were not considered relevant. However, as the process of integration has gained momentum, so have the questions and concerns raised by non-EC members, and it is to these that the EC is increasingly turning its attention.

In considering the EC's posture toward non-Community countries, it is important to recognize the widely accepted view in the EC that the benefits of the program to complete the internal market should accrue to the Community. As a leading Italian industrialist put it, "the single market must first offer an advantage to European companies. This is a message we must insist on without hesitation."[9] A representative of a major French enterprise also asserted that the benefits "should be reserved first and foremost to European firms."[10]

The rationale for this view, which is translated into support for a restrictive policy vis-a-vis nonmember countries, is based on several propositions.

- Since the market-opening measures of the White Paper will entail dislocation and risks for domestic interests exposed to new competitive pressures, it is politically necessary to counterbalance these effects with greater restrictions on outsiders (however defined). In fact, this may be required to obtain sufficient political support for the White Paper proposals.
- The economic counterpart of the above political argument is that it is both appropriate and necessary to provide some measure of protection for a transitional period. As a French industrial leader asserted, "all new groupings started with protection; the EC needs some form of protection." This is propounded both as a general proposition and a "defensive policy" to reduce pressure on firms not yet able to withstand international competitive pressures and on firms with limited adjustment potential.[11]
- Nonmembers should not enjoy the benefits that will accrue to participants inside the Community from completion of the internal market without having to "pay" in some way—in other words, there should be "no free ride." In accordance with this proposition, it is asserted that the Community should withhold market-opening measures resulting from completion of the internal market to obtain reciprocal benefits either bilaterally or in the Uruguay Round of trade negotiations.
- The Community needs to protect itself against competition from the Asian economies and particularly Japan; this has been one of the motivating factors in the Community's effort to complete the internal market.

While all of this adds up to a fairly formidable array of protectionist forces, a number of countertendencies exist. First is the general policy orientation of the Community, enunciated on many occasions, in favor of a liberal economic and trading regime. This position is subscribed to by most member governments, particularly Germany and the United Kingdom, referred to by a Commission official as "the guardians of orthodoxy in the Community."

Support for such a regime reflects the Community's position as the world's leading trading bloc, a position that would be damaged if its trading partners retaliated against the imposition of protectionist measures.

However, the considerations are not based simply on philosophy and retaliatory fears. More important is the conviction among many in the Community that the EC would be the loser if it were to adopt a protectionist policy. They believe that protectionism would entail economic costs and disadvantages to the EC and that the protectionists underestimate the dynamic effects of completing the internal market. In addition, an increasing number of EC enterprises are involved in business activity outside the EC, which they fear could be subject to retaliation as a result of protectionist actions. Hence, in many sectors, an assessment of interests leads to the conclusion that more can be gained through an open economic system—in terms of acquisition of technology, access to markets, ability to participate as part of the global financial network, and potential for participating in international alliances.

A final factor in considering any possible protectionist measures is that the Community will need to take into account its various international obligations, which in many respects will limit the EC's freedom of action. Most obvious are the trade rules set forth in the GATT. In addition, most of the member states have entered into treaties of friendship, commerce and navigation with the United States (and other countries as well). While the provisions vary, they generally provide for national treatment for U.S. firms—or at least treatment equal to that accorded firms of other countries. Finally, there are OECD codes, notably the Codes of Capital Movements and Current Invisible Transactions, that include the right of establishment.

THE GENERAL EC ATTITUDE AND POLICY TOWARD U.S. FIRMS

The general thrust of Community policy affecting the activities of U.S. firms in the EC—exporters and investors—will be influenced to a considerable degree by the context in which EC decisions are taken. Paramount will be the general *economic climate* and the state of the US-EC relationship.

The first great adjustment in the EC was the progressive elimination of customs duties between the member states, concurrent with the establishment of a common external tariff. That transition took place during a period of economic prosperity, which clearly facilitated the process. The adjustments involving creation of an integrated market will similarly cause dislocations. To the extent these occur under conditions of economic growth, the transition will be easier to accomplish. On the other hand, if the EC is facing a period of slow growth, the adjustments and attendant problems will be more severe, thereby increasing the EC's disposition to limit the opportunities for non-EC firms.

No less important will be the nature and mood of *relations between the United States and the Community.* This will be reflected in the first instance in areas such as the existence and seriousness of specific trade disputes as well as the two sides' respective policies and positions in multilateral economic institutions, particularly the Uruguay Round of trade negotiations. But it will also extend to other facets of U.S. trade policy: EC perceptions of U.S. "protectionism" as reflected in trade legislation and actions taken under it as well as any perceived shift from multilateral to bilateral solutions to trade problems adversely affecting the EC.

In addition, the willingness and success of the United States in reducing its trade and budgetary deficits, which the EC will view as necessary in forming the basis for sounder international economic cooperation, will be a relevant factor. To the extent the Community considers the United States to be pursuing "irresponsible policies," it will be more difficult to engage the Community in a harmonious and positive dialogue on internal market issues. Needless to say, however, U.S. and EC perceptions about the appropriateness of U.S. policies may be drastically different. The EC may well find itself in the uncomfortable position of applauding the decline in the U.S. trade deficit, while complaining of the resultant transformation of the EC's trade surplus with the United States into a deficit.

At the same time, the US-EC relationship should not be viewed solely in economic terms, but should take into account the political and security dimensions as well. In particular, Europeans view security as an important element of the relationship, and thus the rising transatlantic debate over European security cannot be entirely divorced from trade issues. As an Italian leader put it, if the EC believes the United States is going its "separate way" on security, the economic relationship will become "more difficult." On the other hand, an economically stronger Community resulting from completion of the internal market should be better able to increase its share of the defense burden, thus reducing possible friction with the United States.

The EC's posture toward the United States will also be affected by two very different types of external relationships: one with Japan and the emerging Asian economies and the other with the European Free Trade Association countries.

The EC's *relationship with Japan* and the industrializing Asian countries is difficult. As discussed, it has been characterized by a rising tide of concern in the Community over the level of Japanese penetration of the EC economy, and to a lesser extent by the newly industrializing Asian countries, as well as over the obstacles facing EC firms seeking to do business in Japan. In large measure, Japan is perceived as representing the greatest threat to the competitive position of the EC, a threat resulting not only from its economic power but also from unfair trading practices. As the EC's frustration with the Japanese has increased, the EC has undertaken aggressive policies in dealing with Japan, manifested, for example, in antidumping actions and pressures to improve market access in Japan. Partially in response—as well as reflecting large balance of payments surpluses—Japanese investment in the EC has risen substantially, a situation viewed with mixed emotions: generally satisfaction for its income and employment-producing effects in the place where the investment is located, and often displeasure by competitors in the EC. Thus, with heightened concern in the Community about competition from and activities by Japan as a major impulse for the program to complete the internal market, the EC will be looking for ways to limit Japan's ability to reap the benefits of the integrated market, or at least to do so without giving something in return. The danger for the United States is that it will be caught, even if unintentionally, in that web.

A corollary of the concern over Japan and the Asian industrializing countries is that a more restrictive policy will become increasingly likely to the extent the EC believes that the benefits of the integrated market are being reaped by "outsiders" rather than within the EC itself. Certainly, Japanese successes in the integrated market would hardly be unexpected.[12]

The *EFTA-EC relationship* is totally different. All the EFTA members have relatively small, healthy economies that are heavily dependent on their trade and economic interaction with the EC. As a bloc, they are the leading trading partner of the Community. Relations between EFTA and the EC have always been close, reflecting geographic proximity, economic, historical, and cultural ties and former EFTA membership by some of the more recent EC member states. For obvious reasons, the EFTA countries have cultivated such a relationship. Each EFTA member has negotiated a free trade agreement with the EC, and all now use the Single Administrative Document (see Chapter 4). In addition, EFTA participates in the European standards bodies (these are European, as opposed to EC, organizations). On the other hand, EFTA does not share the budgetary costs of the Community, nor does it assume legal obligations or have to make political concessions.[13]

But not only is EFTA outweighed by the Community in terms of economic strength, it also is an essentially different kind of organization, lacking any supra-national elements. The institutional structure is considerably weaker and less developed than that of the EC, and decisions can only be taken by unanimity. In addition, the six member states are physically separated and vary considerably in their types of economy and interests.

EFTA's overarching concern about the EC's program to complete the internal market is that there will no longer be roughly comparable access among all European markets;[14] the EC member states will gain better access to each other, and EFTA will join the other "outsider" countries looking in at a more dynamic Community. The specific concerns cover a broad range: that trade will increase inside the integrated market rather than draw in more imports; that EFTA countries will be unable to participate in the EC's R&D projects; that EFTA countries will have to adopt EC-harmonized technical standards to remain competitive; that free movement of labor inside the EC (not applicable to EFTA nationals) will benefit EC firms at EFTA's expense; that an EC common air transportation policy will put EFTA national carriers at a competitive disadvantage; that EC regulations on financial services for institutions operating in the EC could hamper Swiss bank activities; and generally that the Community will outpace EFTA economically.

Not surprisingly, EFTA has continually stressed its close ties with the EC, particularly the formal agreements. The clearest expression was contained in the 1984 Luxembourg Declaration, in which the EC and EFTA ministers stressed the "importance of strengthening cooperation, with the aim of creating a dynamic European space."[15] The concept of a "European space," often quoted by EFTA countries, has not been defined, but rather has been used to describe a sort of special relationship. EFTA recognizes that it cannot participate directly in EC decisionmaking. However, EFTA countries are anxious to influence the EC's deliberations on issues of interest to them. The hope, as stated in a Swedish government report, is that it will be possible to exchange information and consult to arrive at a common solution for all 18 EC and EFTA countries.[16]

EFTA members are also looking for arrangements under which they would be exempt from EC policies toward nonmembers—for example, suggestions have been made that the EC antidumping regulations not apply to EFTA on the grounds that any problems could be covered by the EC competition policy and that a joint EC-EFTA public procurement liberalization should be undertaken. In seeking to enhance its "insider" status, EFTA is well aware that it will need to offer something in return. Some EFTA members have offered to make monetary contributions, for example to the EC's regional development funds or for participation in student exchange programs. However, for the most part, EFTA countries will find it difficult to offer reciprocal treatment in many areas of interest to them—whether it be free movement of people or mutual recognition of banking supervision.

On the EC side, while voicing general recognition of a "special relationship" with EFTA, the Community has shown a clear reluctance to permit EFTA to impinge on the internal deliberations of the decisionmaking process. Indeed, EFTA has been one of the main targets of the "no free ride" rhetoric. A reflection of the EC's concern over the dilution of its authority has been its hesitation to conclude an agreement with Switzerland according reciprocal rights of establishment for nonlife insurance; the EC has feared that it would not be able to change its regulations subsequently without consulting Switzerland. But despite these concerns, there are about 20 bilateral EC-EFTA working groups discussing issues such as banking, telecommunications and transportation, which could lead to some understandings on White Paper issues.

The relevance to the United States of EFTA's efforts is that to the extent EFTA succeeds in obtaining special status in the integrated market, the United States and other nonmembers are placed at a relative disadvantage. On the other hand, if EFTA's efforts result in a more open internal market, all outsiders will gain.

Prospects. The one unambiguous assertion that can be made is that no overall pattern of Community behavior toward outside countries has emerged; indeed, the EC is only now beginning to address the external issues posed by its program to complete the internal market.

At most, two general propositions are relevant.

- The starting point for EC consideration of the external aspects of the integrated market is not a basic predisposition to establish a "Fortress Europe" to the exclusion of outsiders; that does not imply, however, a warm, unquestioned welcome for all who would seek to participate in the market.
- The EC firmly subscribes to the principles of a liberal international economic framework, as enshrined in the GATT, the OECD and other multilateral institutions, because it recognizes the benefits that accrue to it from the global economic system.

However, that level of generality provides few clues as to the attitudes and policies the EC will adopt on specific issues relevant to the United States. As of mid-1988, it is difficult to go farther than to identify the forces and pressures that will determine the outcome of decisions that will be taken over time affecting the operations of U.S. firms, and of other nonmember countries, in the EC. On the one hand, if the process of completing the internal market proceeds as expected, the new dynamism and increased competition will result in dislocations that will create protectionist pressures. This will be compounded by the strong tradition of regulation and protection in much of the EC. On the other hand, a number of factors support an open regime: the constraints of the EC's international obligations; fear of retaliatory action by its economic partners, notably the United States; and, perhaps most important, the belief of many of the economic operators that the EC will derive greater advantages from an open system.

STEPS U.S. FIRMS SHOULD TAKE

U.S. firms presently or potentially doing business in the EC cannot ignore the monumental changes that are taking place inside the European Community. What should they do?

First, *gather information.* Proposals are being debated and decisions taken within the Community that will have direct effects on U.S. business, be it export or investment. It is critical for U.S. firms to know details and current status of these proposals, their prospects, the differing interests involved, and the balance of strength between them. This can be done with varying degrees of intensity. Firms can rely on their offices situated in Brussels or elsewhere in the Community, or they can obtain information through business connections in the EC. Alternatively, they can make use of the 1992 Information Service of the U.S. Department of Commerce.

In addition, a variety of published sources are available. The *Financial Times* of London, printed in the United States, provides the most complete daily coverage of EC news. There are also a number of more specialized Brussels publications on developments inside the EC, notably the *European Report* (published by Europe Information Service) and publications of the EC Committee of the American Chamber of Commerce in Belgium, *Business Guide to EC Initiatives* (semiannual) and *Countdown 1992* (quarterly). Finally, a growing number of firms in the United States and EC are offering information and consultative services. And U.S. trade associations and other business organizations are becoming increasingly able to provide sector-specific information to their members.

Second, *review and develop strategies.* Because each firm's individual situation will differ, generalizations about appropriate actions are meaningless. It is essential, however, for firms to assess the changes taking place in the EC as they may affect their future operations.[17] The degree of detail will depend on the level of actual and potential involvement in the EC. However, all the basic questions have to be asked—how will the integrated market affect corporate structure, size and location of plants, scope for joint ventures and other cross-border activities, capital investment programs, distribution and transportation, purchasing, marketing, staff recruitment and development, computer and telecommunications systems, and scope for standardization.

A fundamental question is whether exporters should consider establishing operations inside the EC. In the abstract, the answer has to be affirmative simply because of the increased business opportunities in the EC and the greater certainty of access for firms physically located in the Community. Obviously, however, choices are never that clear-cut. There will always be powerful reasons for U.S. firms to export, such as size of the exporting firm, size of the potential market relative to the investment cost, nature of the product, and rapidly changing technology. Under virtually all conceivable circumstances, U.S. multinationals in the EC will want to import at least a portion of the components for their European subsidiaries from the United States, and increased investment will indeed most likely lead to a higher level of exports from the United States to the EC. Furthermore, a growing number of U.S. firms will presumably want to take advantage of the export opportunities afforded by the relatively weak dollar.

Third, *influence the decisionmaking process.* This is by no means a simple undertaking. The interests of U.S. firms affected by developments in the EC range from marginal to intense. In addition, the Brussels structure and mode of operation are far different—and less transparent—than those of the United States. Nonetheless, as indicated above, the various EC institutions are becoming increasingly receptive to presentations of views and suggestions by interested, and informed, parties. Access by U.S.-based groups, whether they are a trade association or an enterprise, will remain difficult but not impossible. Perhaps useful dialogues can be established with sustained effort.

On the other hand, U.S. subsidiaries can gain direct access to Commission officials and members of the European Parliament. They can also make their views known through European trade and industry groupings, although a distinctly U.S. perspective will more likely be submerged in the interests of EC enterprises. In addition, there are U.S. business organizations representing a strictly U.S. point of view. These include the EC Committee of the

American Chamber of Commerce in Belgium (representing U.S. subsidiaries in the EC) and the U.S. Industry Coordinating Group, an informal body comprising the U.S. Council on International Business, National Association of Manufacturers, National Foreign Trade Council, and the U.S. Chamber of Commerce. Separately, these and other similar national organizations are becoming increasingly active in promoting U.S. business interests on issues relating to the EC's 1992 program.

NOTES

1. "The real winners in 1992," *Financial Times*, March 10, 1988.
2. In addition, there are a number of special trading relationships, primarily with developing countries, under which one or more member countries agree to import specified quantities of goods, often above the market price.
3. "Renault chief urges protection," *Financial Times*, March 24, 1988.
4. Treaty of Rome, Article 58.
5. COM(85) 310, paragraph 19.
6. Paolo Cecchini, *The European Challenge 1992* (Wildwood House, Aldershot [U.K.], 1988), pp. xix–xx.
7. EC Commissioner Willy De Clerq, quoted in "Looming shadow of Fortress Europe," *Financial Times*, July 14, 1988.
8. Jacques Pelkmans and Alan Winters, *Europe's Domestic Market*, Royal Institute of International Affairs Chatham House Papers No. 63 (London: Routledge, 1988), p. 61.
9. Speech by Umberto Agnelli, Royal Institute of International Affairs, London, April 14, 1988.
10. Elf-Acquitaine representative quoted in *European Report*, No. 1361, November 28, 1987.
11. See "Protectionism - a Necessary Price for Achieving the European Internal Market?," *Intereconomics*, January/February 1987, pp. 9–13.
12. "Japan may make biggest gains from single market," *Financial Times*, June 27, 1988.
13. "Worried Swiss weigh cost of keeping the Community door open," *Financial Times*, March 3, 1988. See also "Piece by piece the jigsaw grows," *Financial Times*, March 23, 1988.
14. Paul Krugman, "EFTA and 1992," Occasional Paper No. 23 (Geneva: European Free Trade Association, June 1988).
15. Joint Declaration of European Community and European Free Trade Association Ministers, Luxembourg, April 9, 1984.
16. Ministry for Foreign Affairs, "Sweden and West European Integration," extracts from Swedish government's bill 1987/88:66, unofficial translation, Stockholm, December 1987.
17. Although prepared for a European audience, a useful guide to company preparations for the integrated market is J.S.N. Drew and E.V. Drew, *Europe 1992: Developing an Active Company Approach to the European Market* (London: Commission of the European Communities, 1988).

A Look at Some Sectors 8

Previous chapters have reviewed the issues involved in completing the internal market; this chapter examines some economic sectors in terms of how U.S. firms operate in the Community, the extent to which they confront barriers among the member countries, and the effect an integrated market will have on their operations and competitive position. The following discussions are not intended to be in-depth studies, but rather to give an indication of the types of situations U.S. firms may face.

AUTOMOBILES

The U.S. automotive presence in the EC is represented by massive, long-standing investments by the two largest U.S. manufacturers. Both established operations in Europe long before World War II, and both have become self-contained companies organized on a pan-European basis with sourcing, design and operations largely coordinated among the European countries (this includes not only the EC but also Western European nonmembers). European operations form a significant component of both companies' worldwide operations and an important contributor to profits. U.S. exports by the "big three" account for a very small share of the EC market, although the U.S. producers are looking to increase this.

The main barriers faced by the automobile companies in the EC relate to taxes and to product standards and regulations. In addition to the different levels of VAT (see Chapter 3), sales and registration taxes are imposed by most member states. These taxes, which are not included in the White Paper's tax harmonization proposals, range from zero in France, Germany and Spain to 180 percent on large cars in Denmark.[1] Another form of competitive distortion is caused by national and local government aid, often substantial, to domestic automobile manufacturers in forms such as grants, loans, equity injections, and debt write-offs.

Equally significant are differences in a number of product standards. Although there are uniform standards covering many automobile features, others remain subject to country-specific unique specifications, such as yellow headlights in France, side repeater-flasher lights in Italy and dim-dip lights in the United Kingdom. Thus, there is no EC-type approval for automobiles, a situation favored by some EC manufacturers, that, out of concern over Japanese competition, want to maintain the differentiation among the EC markets.

But most important are emission standards. Because they affect environmental policy, emission standards are a highly political and highly sensitive subject. Most concerned are the Danes, the Dutch and the Germans, in part because of their experience with acid rain. The effect on the market of different emission controls was recognized early on by the Commission, which has tried for a number of years to coordinate these policies. In 1987, agreement was reached on common standards for larger passenger and commercial vehicles; as of mid-1988, action was blocked on similar standards for smaller passenger vehicles. However, Denmark took the option under the Single European Act to leave its more stringent standards in effect. Germany and the Netherlands have opted to mandate the new standards immediately, while the other member states will delay for several years. The result, of course, will be to perpetuate at least some differences in the EC. In addition, these differences are reinforced by tax incentives offered by some member states for complying with stricter standards than the harmonized levels (for example, the Netherlands in the case of noise level standards).

By all counts, the cost of the fragmented EC automobile market is high. According to one automotive source, it comes to just under $700 per car for an average sized manufacturer.[2] In a study conducted as part of the Cecchini report (discussed in Chapter 5), it was estimated that completion of the internal market could result in savings to the automobile industry of over $6 billion and could bring about a 6 percent increase in demand.[3]

Of course, consumer differences among national markets also play a part in determining manufacturers' output—for example, Germans generally prefer larger cars, and Italians, smaller ones. However, insofar as emission standards are concerned, the options open to manufacturers under the circumstances are to build a limited variety of cars with the most complete emission control equipment or to produce a range of models in accordance with the different emission standards. Because the former option in most cases would adversely affect competitiveness, companies operating in the EC have decided to offer different emission control equipment on most models, depending on the emission standards of the country in which the cars are to be sold. A further relevant fact is the engine size at which more stringent emission standards are imposed. The higher the minimum size, the less that automobile prices will be affected by the different controls.

A potentially important but uncertain factor affecting the EC automobile market after completion of the internal market is the disposition of the various national restrictions on automobile imports (see Chapter 7). If the policies ultimately selected to replace the present restrictions result in a significant increase in automobile imports into the Community, that will increase competition inside the EC and presumably put downward pressure on manufacturers' profitability.

Apart from that slight possibility, the establishment of an integrated market in the EC should decrease costs for automobile manufacturers because they will no longer need to satisfy differences (or as many differences) based on national specifications or special requirements; in addition, they will benefit from the liberalization of capital movements and financial services and the removal of border controls. This consideration will apply to U.S. automobile exporters as well as manufacturers. Exporters of automobile components (for U.S. or EC manufacturers) should benefit from a somewhat larger market with fewer barriers, but their particular circumstances may vary considerably. In any event, the benefits of an integrated market will be available to all manufacturers, whether they are inside or outside the Community.

In the short term, it is likely that the U.S. manufacturers will more than hold their own in the EC market because they have rationalized their operations on a European basis—and thus will be able to take advantage of the opportunities of the single market—whereas EC manufacturers operate mainly from a home base and treat exports outside this base as incremental sales. On the other hand, the longer term prospects for U.S. firms will depend more on European manufacturers' ability to move to a considerably greater pan-European strategy.

BANKS

Along with the entire financial services sector, banking is undergoing a massive and rapid change throughout the world. The distinctions among different types of financial institutions, resulting from long-standing regulation and tradition, are breaking down. New products are constantly emerging, and the variety and complexity of financial operations are increasing apace. Although the distinction between banks and investment houses enshrined in the Glass-Steagall Act in the United States does not exist in most of the EC, banking in the member states has been characterized by a high degree of government regulation and considerable protection of domestic institutions.

Since the formation of the EC—and in many cases predating it—U.S. banks have established branches and subsidiaries in all parts of the Community, a trend accelerated by the growth of Europe as an important financial center. Their degree of welcome and freedom of operation has varied among the EC member states, but on the whole they have developed a strong position in the EC. Most U.S. banks have not sought to enter the retailing banking sector, which is generally more closely regulated and protected, and on the whole more difficult competitively for nonlocal institutions. However, in the commercial banking sector, U.S. banks have played a much larger role, sharing in the opportunities offered to all financial institutions by the growth in financial services.

The most important development on the banking scene is the second banking coordination directive proposed by the Commission in early 1988; the main feature is that any bank duly established in one member country will be able to operate in any of the member countries (see Chapter 4). For the most part, supervision of the bank's operations will be the responsibility of the country of establishment, irrespective of where its activities take place. The directive's intention is not only to diminish the complexity of bank supervision and regulation but also to facilitate and expand the provision of financial services in the EC.

Under the prospective banking regime, U.S. institutions will likely benefit from two major advantages. First, they are geographically broad-based and well experienced in operating across borders, whereas banks of EC member countries have traditionally been strong in their home country and less active regionally. Second, as a result of their U.S. experience, they have generally been, at least until recently, in the forefront of providing innovative services to customers.

Nonetheless, the banking directive contains some features of concern to U.S. banks. To the extent that U.S. banks prefer to continue operating in the EC through branches, which will remain national (rather than EC-wide) institutions, they could find themselves placed at a competitive disadvantage vis-a-vis EC banks (of EC or foreign parentage) since the latter would have to meet only one set of regulations. Second, it is conceivable that regulatory authorities in the member countries (or on an EC level) will assert that home country control cannot in fact be exercised by an EC member state because of the residual supervisory competence exercised by U.S. regulatory agencies over the overseas operations of U.S. banks. However, in view of the increasing cooperation among bank supervision agencies, that is not likely. Finally and most important is the question of reciprocity described in Chapter 7. If the EC were to determine that the United States does not provide reciprocity of treatment and decide to apply the directive to all U.S. banks, regardless of when they were established in EC member states, the competitive position of the U.S. banking industry in the EC would be placed at risk.

Irrespective of how U.S.-specific issues are resolved, it is highly relevant for U.S. banks to consider the changes that will take place—and are beginning to take place—in the EC banking sector. Little change is likely, at least in the short term, in the retail sector since consumer habits and the high cost of establishing (or buying into) a retail network will preclude significant entry of "foreign" banks (either from other member countries or third countries). However, on the wholesale level, important changes are clearly under way. Banks throughout the EC are looking for ways to strengthen their position in what will become a far larger market. Although there have been some in-country mergers (notably Spain), banking has been characterized more by cross-border linkages: purchases, exchanges of stock and other forms of coordinated activity. The net effect will be to enhance the ability of what had essentially been national institutions to operate regionally—and thus to make EC banking more competitive for all participants.

INSURANCE

The insurance sector in the EC consists to a large extent of individual markets in the different member states. Controls over insurance activities in the EC are largely imposed by national authorities who enforce the rules in their country. These regulatory powers vary in degree and form, but in many cases they are considerable. At one extreme is Germany (which accounts for about one-third of EC premium income),[4] where the concept of ensuring that the companies provide adequate protection for the consumers has resulted in a high level of regulation as well as protection against outside (and thus less regulatable) firms. On the other hand, the U.K. insurance industry has been characterized by a considerable degree of self-regulation, although recent passage of the Financial Services Act has introduced a larger role for government than previously. Controls have been greater in the member states on life insurance than on general insurance (property and casualty, fire and related hazards) because the customers are individual consumers, who are deemed to require greater protection than commercial firms.

In many EC countries, the insurance companies are major enterprises, wielding vast economic power. In France and Italy, they are among the largest indigenous firms. In Germany, the five major insurance companies, whose ownership is interlocked with that of industry, are influential players on the economic scene. The U.K. insurance sector, though less concentrated than in some other EC countries, is clearly a world leader, working through the insurance companies and Lloyds of London. Not only are there many insurance companies in the Community (over 3,000), but the individual insurance markets are different in terms of their ways of doing business. In the United Kingdom, for example, the insurance companies operate largely through brokers, which also explains the U.K.'s efforts to participate in the German market by obtaining the right to operate without being physically established there. On the other hand, the pattern in Germany is one of direct dealing by the insurer with the client.

U.S. insurance firms have participated in the EC, although their presence has not been of major proportion. Because of the fragmentation of the market, they have to a great extent operated individually in the separate markets. In each case, they have had to satisfy the relevant national authorities of their conformity with domestic requirements and overcome any informal resistance to their presence in the market, whether they operated through the establishment of their own subsidiaries or through the acquisition of or merger with national companies.

Apart from confirming the principle of freedom of establishment for insurance companies from outside member states and deciding on some ancillary harmonization measures, there was little action on insurance at the Community level until the mid-1980s. This took the form of the decisions of the European Court of Justice at the end of 1986 (see Chapter 2) and Council approval of a directive on nonlife insurance in 1988 (see Chapter 4). The Court's decisions paved the way for an insurance company to sell policies in another member state without being established in that country. Debate over implementation of that decision lasted until early 1988 when the Council approved a directive, which provided that in the case of property and liability insurance for commercial risks over a specified threshold, a company can underwrite insurance in another country (and remain subject to the regulation of the country where it is established).

Thus, the direction of EC policy on insurance is that of reducing national regulatory controls and enabling companies to provide services more easily across national borders. This deregulation is also attracting other financial institutions; for example, the leading banks in both Germany and Italy have indicated an interest in entering the insurance market. At the same time, EC insurance companies have looked increasingly to providing other forms of financial services to the extent permitted by the regulatory authorities. All of this points to considerable movement and change in the insurance sector. Many of the larger firms in the EC are already taking steps to enhance their ability to provide insurance on an EC-wide basis. For example, the largest Italian company sought (unsuccessfully) to acquire a leading French company; that company, in turn, entered into a defensive merger with another French company and bought a British company;

another French insurer bought one-third of Belgium's largest insurer and then agreed to exchange shares with a British insurer; and the largest German (and European) insurance company increased its stake in the U.K. market (but was blocked in its attempt to take over the largest British company).

Overall, the EC insurance market is large, $150 billion,[5] and the level of savings in much of the EC is high. Thus, deregulation of the insurance sector in the EC, with the attendant reduction in the many restrictive practices, should produce new opportunities for market participants—be they U.S., EC or third country firms.

However, although there are no proposals on the table in that regard, the threat remains that the EC will decide to apply reciprocity to the insurance sector on the same terms as are now proposed for banking. In that event, U.S. firms could find their competitive situation jeopardized, since regulation of insurance by the states, rather than the federal government, would presumably prevent the United States from being able to provide conditions of access and operation for EC companies comparable to that proposed in the Community.

MEDICAL DEVICES

The field of medical devices and instruments covers a broad area: active (i.e., electromedical) devices, active implants (e.g., pacemakers), sterile devices (including nonactive implants), and in-vitro diagnostics (tests made outside the body). This is an area of high technology in which U.S. firms are at the vanguard of technological change and where U.S. equipment in many cases is more advanced than that of its competitors. The U.S. industry includes a few very large firms, plus many more medium sized and small ones. It is also relatively new, with improved devices and equipment constantly being developed and produced. By the same token, regulation in the United States came only recently; the U.S. Food and Drug Administration did not begin to set standards for this equipment until the mid-1970s.

While precise figures are not available, the bulk of U.S. sales to the EC appears to come from exports, although the larger U.S. firms have established subsidiaries in the EC for manufacturing and distribution. Even in the latter case, however, a significant portion of sales has consisted of exports from the United States, reflecting the rapidity of technological change and the impossibility (or inefficiency) of placing a substantial part of their research and development and manufacturing in the EC. On the whole, the EC has been receptive to U.S. products in this sector because of their contribution to health care and the relative absence of strong competition from EC firms.

As with the rest of the health sector, governments are deeply involved in the regulation of medical devices. This affects U.S. manufacturers throughout the range of regulation from product registration to certification of conformance with technical standards. Some member states have established technical standards, while others have not—though often in the latter case they are now moving to adopt international standards. More recently, the EC has made a start on instituting EC-wide standards. The result is an array of requirements facing medical device manufacturers. For example, for one U.S. company producing implantable pacemakers for sale in the EC, standards proposed by CENELEC (the European electrical standards body) will eventually have to be met. However, at present they must meet French and Italian standards (for sale in those markets), plus various other regulations and requirements set by Belgium, France, Germany, Italy, the Netherlands, Spain, and the United Kingdom. In addition, there are registration requirements with product testing in France, Germany and Italy; on the other hand, in Belgium, the Netherlands, Spain, and the United Kingdom, registration does not require product testing but rather inspection of the factory and/or process.

Meeting standards is complicated by the fact that products may include components or processes that are subject to technical standards devised for other, more general, purposes. Thus, for example, the external programmer of a heart implant may fall under restrictions on the emission of electromagnetic energy, and a laser used as part of a device may be required to meet other energy emission standards.

Recognizing the benefits of EC-wide standardization, the EC Commission has undertaken to harmonize technical standards in four general areas of medical devices. This effort is being carried out through CEN and CENELEC. Interestingly, the Commission has directly requested the participation of the relevant EC trade associations in this process rather than leaving the task entirely to regulatory experts and/or consumers. U.S. subsidiaries in the EC, hence "EC" firms, are participating in that exercise, though U.S. firms exporting to the EC have more limited access to the standards process, essentially through incipient U.S. trade association efforts.

Medical devices may have to meet not only technical standards but also product testing and certification by recognized bodies. Traditionally, Germany has been considered the premier testing location; its findings have generally been recognized and accepted throughout Europe. Accordingly, as harmonization is developed, Germany may seek to maintain its dominant role in testing. Of particular concern to U.S. firms manufacturing in the United

States and exporting to the EC is whether U.S. testing and certification will be recognized in the EC or whether, as is the case in some member states, these must take place in the EC. If U.S. procedures are not accepted, the adverse effect in terms of cost and time could be considerable.

But member state involvement in the medical devices area goes beyond standards setting. Equally important is government's role as direct and indirect provider of health services: it purchases medical devices, and it reimburses other purchasers. In both activities there is room for member state discrimination in favor of domestic manufacturers of medical devices. Purchasing decisions can favor domestic manufacturers, as can delaying or limiting reimbursement.

For U.S. firms, the implications of completion of the internal market will relate largely to regulations and technical standards. The key consideration for U.S. firms—exporters or investors—will be the nature and scope of the EC regulations and standards ultimately adopted, as well as the testing and certification requirements. Standards harmonization and extension of mutual recognition will facilitate operations in the EC market, although increased regulation to keep pace with technological change could have the opposite effect. On balance, integration of the EC market would seem to present opportunities for U.S. firms to improve their already favorable position in the Community.

PHARMACEUTICALS

Even more than in the case of medical devices, pharmaceuticals is an area of heavy government involvement in all EC countries, first because it concerns fundamental issues of health and safety and second because of the government's role as a provider, or at least funder, of health services. The issues are thus often political and social as much as they are economic. As one observer put it, "pharmaceuticals and politics go together." This is a fact of European life, and there is little reason to expect that it will change appreciably in the near future because it reflects a strong political consensus.

The EC pharmaceutical market is characterized by a large number of manufacturers, represented in virtually all member countries. In Germany alone, there are over 600 manufacturers, the largest of which (also the largest in Europe) accounts for only 6 percent of the market. U.S. pharmaceutical manufacturers are well established in the EC countries (with about 25 percent of the market); the major firms have invested inside the Community (many of them for a long time) and have developed extensive operations throughout the EC. Intense competition takes place through the development and marketing of new products, and to a large extent the customers are government health authorities.

All pharmaceutical companies, U.S. and other, treat the member states as separate markets. To some degree, this is a function of the not insignificant differences among the countries' medical practices and traditions. A more fundamental determinant, however, is the tight control exercised by national governments at all levels of the product cycle. In all countries, this consists of three elements: product registration (in other words, marketing approval); prices (directly or indirectly); and reimbursement to the user (medical facility or patient), the two issues being eligibility for reimbursement and the amount.

Although the various procedures and practices vary by country, a considerable degree of government discretion is involved. Above all, most decisionmaking systems lack transparency, which leaves the way open to national authorities to discriminate in favor of national companies. In some cases, government approval, more favorable prices and/or timely decisions will be enhanced to the extent that the manufacturers' operations are carried out in the country in question. Until recently, France, for example, required that product formulation (i.e., putting it into pharmaceutical form such as tablets and capsules) take place in France. More frequently, the level of employment, exports and/or R&D activity carried out in the country is perceived to affect government decisions relating to individual companies. A further complication is the fact that different government authorities are often involved in making the various decisions that affect the manufacturers' operations. In Belgium, for example, the Ministry of Health decides on registration, the Ministry of Economic Affairs on prices and the Ministry of Social Affairs on reimbursement, each taking action independently of the other.

The first step, that of registration or approval of a product, is generally considered the most scientifically determined and is the least affected by nontechnical considerations. Nonetheless, U.S. firms contend that in some countries the process leaves much to be desired regarding the efficacy of certain products produced by domestic companies and the relative amount of time required for registration (especially in southern member states). Irrespective of the validity of such concerns, the administrative and financial burden of having generally to seek up to 12 separate registrations is obviously heavy.

In virtually all EC member countries, the government maintains price or profit control for pharmaceutical products. Government methods to control prices vary, but all contain a substantial element of administrative discretion. To some extent, the allocation of R&D costs has been a subject of contention for U.S.

firms, as has the issue of price transparency among subsidiaries. In any event, the discretionary and often opaque nature of the process has led some U.S. firms to consider themselves the object of less favorable treatment than that accorded domestic firms. To the extent that domestic manufacturers are accorded higher prices for their products than warranted—an allegation very difficult to prove—they are in effect the recipients of a subsidy. An overriding factor affecting both price and reimbursement decisions is the budgetary pressure facing governments, which has reinforced their efforts to hold down pharmaceutical prices.

As in the case of medical devices, the government's control over reimbursement for purchases of pharmaceuticals can play a crucial role in the ability and desire of a manufacturer to market a certain product—to say nothing of its profit level. The cost of virtually all pharmaceutical products is reimbursed by one means or another—directly by government agencies or indirectly through social insurance schemes. The two government decisions are whether a product will be eligible for reimbursement and, if so, the amount of reimbursement. These decisions are normally separate from that of determining prices and leave considerable room for administrative discretion.

The Commission has initiated a number of actions in the pharmaceutical area, dating back to the first directive (approved in 1965), which requires that medicinal products must be approved by the appropriate authority in the member state and that certain particulars must appear on the label. Amendments to this framework directive 10 years later established a Committee for Proprietary Medicinal Products and provided for partial mutual recognition of product registration. In 1983, in a further directive, the EC instituted a system for multistate registration of pharmaceuticals. That system was recently amended in an attempt to encourage its use.

The 1985 White Paper listed 12 directives relating to pharmaceuticals it considered necessary as part of the package for completing the internal market. Of these, 5 had previously been introduced. The proposed directives covered, among other areas, testing, price transparency and, for completion by 1990, the all-important "work eliminating obstacles to free circulation of pharmaceutical products." In 1987, the EC adopted a package of measures establishing EC-wide rules for biotechnology products (available also for other products) and the protection of rights for data exclusivity for the product originator for a specified time period.

At present, the two main issues on the table are EC-wide registration and the transparency of pricing and reimbursement. Although there is a consensus on the need to replace individual country registration procedures, no agreement has been reached on whether to expand the existing procedures to provide for some form of mutual recognition or whether to establish an EC-wide procedure or institution like the U.S. Food and Drug Administration. Work is farther along on price and reimbursement transparency. A directive proposed by the Commission is presently under consideration by the Council and Parliament. The directive would require fair, objective and verifiable prices, with the onus on member states to give fair and objective reasons for price and reimbursement decisions. Industry would be provided with an appeals mechanism.

Virtually all U.S. firms participating in the EC market have established subsidiaries there and thus can claim status as EC firms. In that capacity they are able to seek to influence the EC political process. Some U.S. firms derive benefits from the fragmentation of the EC market, to the extent their more flexible and extensive operations permit them to fill particular niches. However, all U.S. firms, and EC and third country companies, will stand to benefit from completion of the internal market in terms of opportunities for economies of scale and rationalization of operations. Nonetheless, it is unlikely that any significant rationalization will take place as long as price controls and reimbursement systems remain unchanged.

It is not certain that U.S. firms will have any particular relative advantage over other market participants, although some observers consider the U.S. firms potentially the main beneficiaries because of their extensive coverage of the individual markets. In any event, companies broadly represented throughout the EC, with operations in several countries, may find it difficult as a practical matter to disengage from certain localities in an effort to rationalize their operations.

TELECOMMUNICATIONS

In many respects, telecommunications and the increasingly interrelated field of information technology lie at the heart of economic progress. Together, they constitute a highly complex area that cannot be adequately covered in a few pages. However, since the actions taken by the EC in this sector will have a profound effect on its efforts to improve its competitiveness in an increasingly interdependent world, it is worthy of at least cursory notice.

The telecommunication market is usually divided into four parts: network equipment (transmission and switching); terminal equipment (in the customer's premises attached to the network); basic services (as defined by the individual country but normally including at least voice communications); and enhanced or value-added services (which use the network to manipulate information in a variety of ways—this is the point of convergence between telephone systems and data processing). Telecommunications is an area of intense competition—among companies and products—as well as constant and revolutionary change in technology. Massive investment is required for development of products whose life-cycle is constantly diminishing as successor products are developed.

It is particularly in this sector that forces within the EC have felt the Community was falling behind in the competitive race with the United States and Japan; accordingly, they have emphasized the urgency of creating the conditions under which the EC could develop a viable Community-wide industry capable of holding its own in the world market. The consequences of market fragmentation in the EC have been clear to all observers. The Cecchini report estimated the cost of duplicative standards and restricted public procurement at as much as $6 billion out of a $20 billion market.[6] Perhaps more graphic is the reported expenditure of $10 billion to develop 10 telephone switching systems to meet different national standards, compared with $3 billion spent by three U.S. companies to develop a common system and $1.5 billion to do the same in Japan.[7]

As it became increasingly clear that market fragmentation and government controls over the telecommunication systems in the member countries were the cause of these massive costs, a consensus developed on the necessity for deregulation and the integration of the separate telecommunication markets. Pressures for change came from all sides—the range of manufacturers and users. Possibly contributing as well was pressure from the United States, both in the proposed legislation to limit access to the U.S. market to reciprocal access abroad (though opposed by the Reagan Administration) and the initiation of a dialogue with some of the member states on telecommunications. The Commission set about to study the alternatives and in early 1987 issued a Green Paper on developing a common market in the EC for services and equipment.[8]

This discussion paper laid out the views of the Commission and served as the focus for consideration of the issues by interested parties in the Community. As mentioned in Chapter 3, this paper is not formally connected with the White Paper and thus is not part of the program to complete the internal market. On the other hand, it too has set a completion date of 1992, and its thrust and scope closely parallel those of the White Paper. The extent to which it is successful will significantly influence the success, or lack thereof, of the EC's internal market program.

The Green Paper covers a broad range of issues. It calls for national authorities to continue to provide the network infrastructure and to maintain exclusivity over "indispensable public services" (it being presumed that this would include provision of the user's first telephone). However, the authorities would have to ensure interoperability throughout the EC (through access and interconnections to the network). Other services, particularly value-added services, would be opened to competition. In those areas where the national authority provides services in competition with the private sector, it would have to clearly separate these operations from regulatory functions and prevent the possibility of cross-subsidization with the other activities in which it retained a monopoly. The Green Paper also called for unrestricted access by suppliers to the terminal equipment market—but, significantly, not the network infrastructure—and the establishment of a new standards organization in which users and manufacturers as well as national authorities would be represented.

The proposals of the Commission represent a fundamental change in the EC telecommunication scene, when changes are already taking place in individual member states. In varying degrees, most member states are moving toward deregulation, particularly with respect to terminal equipment and value-added services. At the same time, EC manufacturers have recognized that they need a broader market than that provided by one member state or the EC, and users have recognized the competitive disadvantage to them from limited access to the latest equipment and services. Under the circumstances it was perhaps not surprising that the Green Paper met with a wide degree of acceptance; the debate has related more to implementation and detail.

Nonetheless, the proposed changes threaten a deeply implanted system. At least until recently, each member state has operated its telecommunication system through a government monopoly. Perhaps the most extreme example of vested interests is in Germany, where the roughly 500,000 employees of the Post, Telephone and Telegraph constitute a powerful political force resisting change. At stake are prestige, power and jobs (though some of that only indirectly, since the majority of PTT employees are involved in activities other than telecommunications). Nevertheless, as one observer put it, "the PTT's have lost the war." Even in Germany they seem to have resigned themselves to inevitable change, albeit grudgingly. Possibly indicative was the visit to the United States in 1988 of a high-level German PTT team to conduct seminars for potential U.S. bidders on how to supply to the German market. Such a visit, however, will not in itself convince U.S. companies that they will have an equal opportunity to compete in the German market—not an inconsequential consideration when, for example, it costs about $200 million to reconfigure a network switch to meet German specifications.

After receiving and assessing public comments on its Green Paper, the Commission moved forward in 1988 by laying out an ambitious program for putting its proposals into effect.[9] The first step was issuance of a directive providing for the liberalization of the terminal equipment market, surprisingly including the first telephone, under which national authorities will lose their exclusive powers over the supply of terminal equipment by the end of 1990. Although the directive was discussed by the member states, it became effective automatically upon publication by the Commission under a controversial procedure. The second step will be a directive, expected later in 1988, concerning public procurement of network equipment, which will provide for "fair and open" procedures and transparency. Third, another directive will provide for opening up the service market starting in 1989. Finally, a directive will be introduced for the first stage of the mutual recognition of testing and certification.

The United States has an enormous stake in the future development of the EC telecommunication market. U.S. interests cover the range from equipment manufacturers to service providers. Their ability to participate in this market will be a significant factor in the relationship between the United States and the EC. The issues of concern to U.S. interests largely boil down to access to the market for suppliers of equipment and services. More specifically, they essentially fall under the headings of standards and procurement.

Telecommunications is one of the areas specifically exempted from EC regulations on public procurement (see Chapter 4), and despite the Commission recommendation of a few years ago that member states open 10 percent of their national telecommunication markets to nonnational firms, the market has been characterized by national government attentiveness to the interests of "national champions." That has certainly been the case with network equipment; the situation has been similar for terminal equipment and value-added services purchased by national authorities in the member states. The latter are particularly important because they represent the areas of greatest potential growth.

To a large extent, U.S. suppliers of equipment and services have established subsidiaries in the EC and thus qualify as EC firms. Although they have not fared well in competition with the "national champions," their prospects should improve with the diminution of the role of national authorities. One likely effect over time of opening the public procurement market will be a shakeout of overcapacity in the network equipment industry, where the existing eight or nine producers will in all probability be reduced by market forces to a maximum of three, thus decreasing the number of "champions." Insofar as U.S. exporters are concerned, a further opening of the telecommunication market would appear to depend on the timing and nature of any renegotiation of the GATT procurement code, where reciprocal benefits would undoubtedly be demanded by the EC.

But the nub of the problem for U.S. interests is standards, which cause supplying firms to face a series of individual, differentiated markets. Although for some products the absence of EC-wide standards can enable a supplier to find markets that might otherwise not be available, on the whole they clearly represent a barrier. The situation should be improved by the recent establishment of the European Telecommunications Standards Institute, following a proposal in the Green Paper. This is a step forward because it will end the monopoly of the 26-nation Conference of European Administrations of Posts and Telecommunications (CEPT) over the standards process by including participation by manufacturers.

The outcome for U.S. firms will depend on developments in three key areas:

- The extent to which U.S. firms are able to participate in the standards-setting process and, related to that, the degree of transparency. There is some reason for optimism. CEPT recently submitted proposed standards to U.S. manufacturers for comment, although U.S. interests were not involved earlier in the process and it is not clear how much influence their comments will ultimately have.
- Whether testing and certification at U.S. facilities will be recognized in the EC, a question that remains open.
- The extent to which European, as opposed to international, standards are adopted (see Chapter 7). This can be particularly important in that a different European system could raise the cost of access for U.S. products, while creating benefits for a hitherto fragmented EC market. It can also make it more difficult to arrive at global standards in the International Telecommunications Union.

One recent and rather surprising success of the EC on telecommunication standards setting was the decision—reached in early 1987 after only four months of deliberations—on standards for cellular telephones. These were to be phased in over a several-year period to make equipment compatible throughout the EC, in place of the "splendid example of European market balkanisation."[10] However, the number of products in the telecommunication and information technology field is almost infinite, and

118   THE 1992 CHALLENGE FROM EUROPE

the EC will have to put into effect procedures for removing inter-country barriers across a whole range of issues if it is to maximize the benefits of an integrated market in this area.

NOTES

1. "The Cost of Non-Europe," *Motor Industry Review*, No. 1, August 1987, p. 262.
2. Ibid., p. 267.
3. "EC single market promises major savings for the Community's motor industry," *Financial Times*, May 18, 1988.
4. Federal Insurance Association, Bonn.
5. "Europe's insurance map redrawn," *The Economist*, July 9, 1988, pp. 71–72.
6. Paolo Cecchini, *The European Challenge 1992* (Wildwood House, Aldershot [U.K.], 1988), p. 53.
7. "Making Europe a Mighty Market," *The New York Times*, May 22, 1988.
8. "Summary Report concerning the Green Paper on the Development of the Common Market for Telecommunications Services and Equipment," XIII/197 (87), May 26, 1987.
9. "Towards a Competitive Community-Wide Telecommunications Market in 1992," COM(88) 48, February 9, 1988.
10. "EC seeks to end parochialism in telecommunications," *Financial Times*, July 11, 1988.

Implications for U.S. Policy 9

The evolution of the European Community into an integrated market not only presents opportunities and challenges to the U.S. business community, but it also raises issues that will require the attention of U.S. policymakers. However, governments traditionally focus on issues requiring immediate attention and resolution; they tend not to look ahead and anticipate problems. The U.S. government is no exception and has thus found it difficult to deal with the EC's internal market program. The target is indistinct as well as shifting. The issues raised are mainly prospective rather than immediate, and it is premature to conclude whether, and if so to what extent, the Community will adopt measures diminishing the ability of U.S. firms to compete inside the EC.

Nonetheless, the changing situation will need to be watched closely for possible effects on U.S. interests and policies. In fact, the U.S. government has begun to address specific issues with the EC.

Before reviewing the areas requiring U.S. government attention, it is important to emphasize that the development of a stronger, more dynamic European Community is in the U.S. interest. In our economically interdependent world, all nations benefit from the prosperity of the others. Increased EC economic growth, with its attendant increase in demand and production, will be a plus for the United States. However, this development should also be viewed in its political and security aspects. As the EC achieves greater cohesiveness and strength, it is better able to play a positive role in the international community and to increase its contribution to the common defense, and that promotes basic U.S. policy objectives.

SPECIFIC ISSUES FACING THE UNITED STATES

Import quotas. At some point, the EC must decide whether to phase out member state import quotas or to transpose them to a Community-wide basis. To the extent the EC opts for the latter alternative—highly likely, as indicated in Chapter 7—the trade effects will have to be calculated by the countries exporting to the Community. Unless quotas that now apply to specific exporting countries are made applicable to all sources in that process, the direct U.S. trade interest will presumably remain slight. However, the sector where difficulties could arise is automobiles, in that an EC quota on Japanese vehicles could impinge on U.S. exports or indirectly affect U.S. interests by increasing the level of Japanese imports into the United States. In any event, if any trade damage is suffered, the United States will have to seek compensation under the provisions of the GATT.

National treatment. This is an important principle for the United States as a nation with major foreign investments. In view of the clear reluctance within the Community to embrace national treatment unambiguously (as it is stipulated in the Treaty of Rome), thus implying less than equal treatment for U.S. firms in the EC, it is important that the United States be attentive to EC policies in this area and be prepared to respond forcefully if the situation requires. At the same time, the willingness and ability of the U.S. Administration to deflect pressures in the United States for similar derogations from national treatment—for example, by imposing controls on foreign investment—will affect the impact of any representations made to the Community.

Reciprocity. The increasing fascination in the EC with reciprocity as a means of obtaining maximum gains in non-EC countries from the development of an integrated market is troubling and troublesome. As outlined in Chapter 7, this is potentially the most vexatious issue for the United States as U.S. interests would be adversely affected.

The issues involved are both legal and practical. The basic principle governing trade negotiations—followed by the GATT contracting parties, including the United States and the EC member states—has been to seek an overall balance of concessions among the negotiating partners. Equality of treatment in individual sectors of the economy has not been sought. The conditions of access or operation in different sectors vary among countries for a variety of reasons, and any effort to match these would necessarily limit the gains that could be negotiated.

However, this principle applies to trade in goods, whereas the EC's prospective use of reciprocity would be in other areas where there are no relevant GATT provisions. Indeed, the EC has very clearly made this distinction. As EC Commissioner De Clerq said recently, "Where international obligations do not exist . . . we see no reason why the benefits of our internal liberalization should be extended unilaterally to third countries. We shall be ready and willing to negotiate reciprocal concessions with third countries."[1]

It is incumbent on the U.S. government to review carefully other international obligations of the EC for possible conflicts with the imposition of reciprocity requirements. One set of agreements worth particular study is the treaties of friendship, commerce and navigation with most of the individual member states, which in almost all cases provide for national treatment or at least most-favored-nation treatment. It should be noted that these were entered into before the establishment of the EC, hence the question arises of whether—and if so how—they are affected by obligations assumed by EC member states as a consequence of their membership in the Community.

There is a further legal consideration: would the EC be justified in imposing obligations on its trading partners arising from domestic (intra-EC) measures opening up the EC economy, which were not the result of negotiations with the other countries. In effect, it is the same question as that posed by deregulation of the U.S. telephone system: can EC companies benefit from measures taken domestically in the United States—and for reasons unrelated to U.S. trade and other economic relations—or can U.S. actions create obligations for the EC? The latter view was reflected in the provision included in the U.S. draft 1988 trade legislation (subsequently modified) that access to the U.S. telecommunication market would be restricted to countries providing comparable access (a provision, incidentally, opposed by both the U.S. Administration and the EC).

The response of the EC to expressions of concern is that the concept of reciprocity is justified on the basis of equity (i.e., obtaining something in return for completion of the internal market) and as a legitimate bargaining strategy in the Uruguay Round of trade negotiations (i.e., using the market opening as leverage to obtain concessions). The legal arguments against reciprocity available to the United States are by no means conclusive. To the extent similar policies are adopted, or at least proposed, in the United States, those arguments will tend to be undercut. The issue has arisen in the United States in connection not only with telecommunications but also with financial services. In its original version, the 1988 trade legislation prohibited foreign companies from acting as dealers of primary securities in the United States if U.S. firms did not enjoy a similar right in the foreign country in question (a clause aimed at restrictions in Japan). As ultimately approved, however, the restriction was softened to require national treatment.

The arguments against reciprocity may be more effective if made on pragmatic grounds. As the Deputy Secretary of the Treasury stated in an official U.S. government pronouncement on the EC's internal market, there will always be differences, at least in the financial sector, in areas such as organizational structures, scope of permitted operations and the regulatory and prudential frameworks.[2] Conducting international economic relations on the basis of reciprocity is not in the long-term interest of the EC any more than it is in that of the United States. The result would be a limitation in the flexibility of the market and in the advantages derived by all participants.

But most powerful may be the threat of a "U.S. response" to the imposition of reciprocity requirements. An effective counter would certainly be the threat of instituting reciprocity requirements in the United States in one or more of the many areas where the more open U.S. system provides facilities not available to U.S. firms in the EC.

A specific sectoral area where important U.S. interests are at stake—and where in fact the U.S. government is already actively engaged in a dialogue with the EC—is access to the expanding EC *telecommunication* market.

Four issues, less readily apparent, could also become contentious. The first is *exports from Japanese investments in the United States* to the EC. It is highly likely that the level of Japanese investment will increase in the coming years, both as a result of the high yen and of real or perceived trade restrictions in the United States. While some of these plants have already begun to export, primarily to Asia, it is quite probable that the level of such exports will rise substantially in the coming years (see Chapter 7). The EC could become an increasingly attractive export destination because of the exchange rates and as a means of avoiding EC pressures or measures to reduce imports from Japan. Thus, the United States could become embroiled in a dispute with the EC over the "origin" of these exports; in the continued absence of an international understanding on rules of origin, this could prove difficult to resolve.

A second "sleeper" issue relates to *U.S. export control* legislation and policy. Thus far, export control matters have been handled by the individual EC countries in conformity with the national security provisions of the Treaty of Rome. However, conflicts have arisen between the United States and certain EC member states as a result of U.S. efforts to enforce unilateral U.S. export controls on high technology products to particular destinations—these are controls other than those agreed to by the industrialized democracies in the Coordinating Committee on Multilateral Export Controls (COCOM). Specifically, the United States has sought to exercise extraterritoriality—jurisdiction in foreign countries—in controlling re-exports of certain high technology products from member states. At such time as the EC's internal barriers are removed, re-exports of U.S. products and other export control issues will become a Community, rather than a member state, matter. This will mean that the United States will have to deal with the Commission, which may or may not

prove to be understanding of U.S. security policies and imperatives; it will also mean that weaknesses in the export controls of
some member states could require a tightening of the U.S. control system applying to the EC as a whole.

Third, the United States may also face *cultural barriers* in the
development of an EC broadcasting regime. As indicated in Chapter 7, a recurring theme of efforts to broaden the radio and television broadcast area and harmonize operating conditions is that
a greater portion of EC-produced material should be included. Although usually couched in terms of expanding the Community's
cultural development, these proposals are clearly aimed at reducing the share of programming from the United States.

Finally, the development of a common *civil aviation* policy directed from Brussels, if and when achieved, would presumably
involve creation of a single entity for the negotiation of bilateral
agreements; thus, the United States would be expected to conclude agreements with the Community rather than the member
states. As a result, rights presently enjoyed by some U.S. carriers to transport passengers between EC countries would, in EC
eyes, relate to internal travel, which is not open to foreign carriers. Since the same limitation applies in the United States, the
EC could seek to revoke those U.S. rights or demand "equal treatment" in the United States. That would adversely affect the balance of advantages and clearly call for a sharp response.

CONFLICTS WITH THE URUGUAY ROUND

A final, crucial area of concern for U.S. public policy is the
relationship between the process of completing the internal market and the ongoing Uruguay Round of trade negotiations under
the GATT. The United States has placed high priority on successful conclusion of these negotiations, considering them critical for
U.S. interests as well as for those of the other trading nations.
Not only is there an economic imperative for actions that will
contribute to a reduction in the huge U.S. trade deficit, but there
is also a political imperative for the U.S. Administration (present
and future) to be able to show its domestic constituency that it
is seeking to improve the international trade framework.

However, there is a potential conflict between the program to
complete the internal market and the Uruguay Round of negotiations in terms of timing and content. The multilateral negotiations
are scheduled to conclude by 1990 (which may or may not happen), while the target date for the internal market is the end of
1992. Many of the issues that are or will be under negotiation
in the Uruguay Round are the subject of action under the White
Paper. The danger from the U.S. perspective is that a conflict

between these two exercises will delay or even block the negotiations. Of particular concern to the United States is the service sector, which the United States made a concerted and successful effort to place on the Uruguay Round agenda. If it should prove impossible to negotiate a code on trade in services before completion of the internal market, the trade round could be put at risk.

One fact must be made absolutely clear: to the extent there is a conflict between completing the internal market and the Uruguay Round or it becomes necessary to set priorities, the integrated market will come first for the Community. The question is whether such a conflict does or might exist. It is by no means evident at this stage that such is the case. On the whole, the program to complete the internal market is a more ambitious and extensive undertaking than is the scope of the GATT negotiations. On services, for example, the Uruguay Round involves as a first step the negotiation of a "framework agreement" of general principles, to be followed in stages by more specific sectoral agreements. At least on the face of it, the EC should find it possible to conclude a framework agreement without feeling hampered in making more detailed internal market decisions in specific service areas. However, the EC has stressed its intention to use as negotiating leverage the market-opening measures it is undertaking as part of its program to complete the internal market, and the main issue in services is access to markets. Accordingly, the possibility exists that the EC will delay Uruguay Round agreement on services so as not to give up the bargaining chip of controlling access to the EC.

As for other negotiating areas, work is less advanced on trade-related investment measures, and the United States and the EC broadly agree on intellectual property (although conflict between the developed and developing countries makes progress uncertain); thus, it is more difficult to foresee a conflict with the internal market exercise. The United States will have a strong interest in negotiations on the GATT procurement code, which could represent an effective avenue for opening up the EC market to U.S.-based, as opposed to EC-based, American companies. However, any expansion of the EC's public procurement market beyond the Community will undoubtedly occur solely on the basis of reciprocity (in this instance, a concept that the United States will find hard to contest).

From a U.S. perspective, two additional potential dangers of a more general nature exist in connection with the Uruguay Round of negotiations. First, the EC's decisionmaking procedures are such that, once the EC sets its internal rules and regulations, it is very difficult to change them. Thus, in cases where EC decisions run counter to proposed GATT solutions, the EC is likely to argue that its positions cannot be changed, hence the other negotiators must accommodate it. This problem is inherent in the nature of the Community; it exists in international negotiating contexts other than the GATT. The second danger is that the EC, in giving precedence to the internal market program, will impede progress in the Uruguay Round by devoting less thought and resources to it than to the internal market. Thus far at least, that does not appear to be the case.

HOW SHOULD THE U.S. GOVERNMENT DEAL WITH THE EC?

U.S. policy must focus not only on the issues, but also on the best method for influencing the EC on internal market issues. It is relevant that, to a considerable extent, the Community is looking to the United States as a model for its efforts. The United States is viewed as a successful example of a single economic unit covering a vast expanse of geography and population, nonetheless with significant powers and roles left to the states. Recognizing the difference between the U.S. experience of having developed such a system more or less from the beginning and the EC's intention to impose one on a number of highly developed and long-established member states, many official and private Europeans have looked to the U.S. experience for guidance. Consequently, the EC is more open than it might otherwise have been to U.S. opinions and points of views, which should facilitate the dialogue on the internal market.

Ability to influence decisions on the internal market presupposes an awareness of the proposals being considered inside the Community as well as access to the decisionmakers. The strongly held view in Washington—which is not limited to internal market issues—is that interested parties are unable to exercise a significant input into decisions because the EC's process is not sufficiently transparent and the U.S. government and private sector do not have sufficient access to decisionmakers at an early enough stage in internal EC deliberations. Too often, it is asserted, by the time that issues come to U.S. attention, decisions have been taken or proposals have proceeded too far to be altered significantly.

To some extent, this view reflects differences in philosophy and tradition between the United States and the EC—in other words, a U.S. assumption, explicit or implicit, that the EC should adopt U.S. decisionmaking procedures. In EC eyes, U.S. concerns are overstated. The U.S. government and private sector are free to consult and discuss issues with the EC at any time, and, in the EC view, both have remained remarkably well informed about activities inside the Community. Neither, the EC adds, have they shown any reticence to raise issues with the EC.

In general, the U.S. government, and to a large extent the private sector (U.S. firms based in the EC), have enjoyed considerable access to the Commission and other EC institutions. The dialogue has been intense and on the whole productive. The U.S. government has been well informed about developments inside the Community. Nonetheless, U.S. interests would clearly be served by greater access to policy considerations within the Commission. Despite the close relationship, on many occasions the United States was not aware of actions being contemplated, and once it found out, the process was difficult to influence.

In any event, there are clear indications that the decisionmaking process in Brussels is becoming more open. More U.S.-style lobbying is taking place at all EC levels, not only with the Commission but incipiently with the Parliament. That should facilitate the ability of the U.S. government, as well as U.S. private interests, to affect the outcome of deliberations of the Community.

A final consideration on U.S. dealings with the EC relates to the evolving relationship between Brussels and the member states. There has always existed a degree of tension between the Commission and the member states, with the Commission seeking to limit the member states' influence over—and even knowledge of—its internal processes. Apart from that, however, over time more and more decisions will be taken in Brussels—through interaction among the Commission, Council and Parliament—and the Commission will acquire authority or at least influence in an increasing number of areas. Over the years, the U.S. government has adopted different modes of dealing with Brussels and the member states. In the early days of the EC, the United States made a conscious effort to support the authority of the Commission and, as a result, tended to concentrate its attention on the Commission in carrying out a dialogue on EC issues. More recently, the United States has raised EC issues with both Brussels and the member governments, often looking to one or more member countries as "allies" on a particular issue and as the best means of influencing the deliberations within the EC.

Almost by definition, U.S. interests are best served by a judicious balancing of dealings with the member states and Brussels—the latter probably including Parliament to an increasing extent. The appropriate mix will have to be based on an assessment of three factors. First, which states can be most helpful on a particular issue, either in terms of providing information or influencing decisions in Brussels—bearing in mind that it is contrary to the interests of these countries to appear to be acting as a surrogate for the United States. Second, what will be the input into decisions of the various Brussels institutions (particularly the Commission but also Parliament as its role changes) under the circumstance of the shift of power from the member states to Brussels. Third, how will the sensitivities of Brussels and the member states be affected by a particular mode of operation by the United States and, in turn, how might that affect the outcome. Obviously that assessment will not be an easy task, but rather will call for considerable diplomatic skills by the U.S. government.

NOTES

1. "1992: the Impact on the Outside World," speech by EC Commissioner Willy De Clerq, Europaeisches Forum, Anspach, August 29, 1988.
2. "The European Community's Internal Market Program: An American Perspective," speech by Deputy Secretary of the Treasury M. Peter McPherson, Institute for International Economics, Washington, August 4, 1988.

Conclusions

The European Community has embarked on an ambitious and broad-ranging attack on the barriers to the existence of a true Common Market, a task set forth by its founding fathers over three decades ago. Although many of the issues and specific proposals had been under consideration for many years, they had never been addressed as part of a comprehensive program; nor had formal approval been given at the highest political level to achieve these measures. Now, however, the Community is committed to "complete" the internal market as it never was in the past.

It is undeniable that the process has begun, and it is clearly irreversible. Even though doubt and disbelief—often not misplaced—have greeted many of the EC's initiatives over the years, the program to complete the internal market has achieved momentum. At some indeterminate point between late 1987 and early 1988, the mood shifted in the Community from hope to certainty. It is no longer a question of "whether," but rather of "how soon" and "how far." Whatever the answers, progress made thus far will not be undone in the future.

The process under way promises a fundamental transformation of the European Community—an even greater change than its formation and the subsequent removal of the internal tariff barriers between member states. To the extent it is successful, completion of the internal market will result in a far more powerful and dynamic economic unit than has existed up to now.

Beyond this point it is risky to be categorical. The enthusiasm—if not euphoria—in the EC about the internal market program must be tempered by recognition of the obstacles to its early realization. Not far beneath the surface lie fears, problems and resistance. Just as the changes inherent in the program will be far-reaching, so will be the upheaval to enterprises, social groups and political forces. That will provoke opposition—some direct, but much of it taking indirect forms—which will not only delay progress in some areas, but also increase the likelihood that formal decisions will be carried out with varying degrees of effectiveness. The record of implementation and enforcement in the Community has been mixed, and there is no reason to expect that these will be miraculously improved. Backsliding can be rectified by administrative and judicial action, but such action takes time. In sum, the system will probably be characterized by uneven progress and perhaps some turmoil as well.

But what does completing the internal market really mean? The Commission has set out a list of specific measures, which officially constitute completion of the internal market. In a sense, completion is both more and less than that list. Indeed, it will be difficult to determine a point at which the internal market has been "completed." Rather, it will be an ongoing process, with no rigidly fixed goal. The U.S. experience shows that an "integrated market" can include a number of differences and barriers among its constituent parts and that there are few unalterable essential elements.

As the process proceeds, the U.S. business community would like short, decisive answers to its many legitimate questions. Unfortunately, no such answers exist—not in terms of what will happen, how their interests will be affected, what they should be doing, and with whom and how to deal. The situation is in flux. Decisions are being taken, and general attitudes and policies are being developed in the Community. These will result from the interaction among numerous groups and individuals, both in government and the private sector. There is no single, unambiguous way of obtaining the facts, ascertaining what is in store, influencing the process, and/or discovering the optimum strategy for dealing with the future.

What is clear is that opportunities await the participants in the EC market. It is hard to foresee that movement toward an integrated market will produce anything other than a higher level of economic activity and a more efficient economic environment.

To a very considerable extent, U.S. firms should be able to operate in the Community on equal terms with other firms, be they EC or non-EC in origin. But it will not all be clear sailing. Competition will be stronger as other firms seek to take advantage of the single market, and some discrimination, overt and covert, will undoubtedly occur. Efforts will be made to distinguish between "local" and "foreign" firms and to give preference to the "local" companies. However, over time this distinction will become increasingly blurred as ownership and interests cross borders, whether intra-EC or external.

The role of the U.S. government will be to monitor the process closely to ensure that U.S. business interests are able to compete on an equal basis. The government has begun to turn its attention to "Europe 1992." However, it is essential that its effort be intensified, that greater resources be devoted to the task, that attention be focused on the issue at the highest levels, and—

by no means least important—that a clear division of responsibilities among the many, often competing government agencies be established. A positive strategy such as this will enable the government to defend U.S. interests as Europe moves to a new era.

Appendix Tables A–D

APPENDIX A. MOST IMPORTANT U.S. MERCHANDISE EXPORTS
TO EC, BY SECTOR, 1982-87*
(Mill. $)

	1982	1983	1984	1985	1986	1987	% Growth 1982-87
Office mach. & ADP equip.	4,777	5,527	6,683	6,443	6,964	8,330	74
Other transport equip.	2,702	3,142	2,837	3,517	4,225	5,144	90
Electrical mach.	2,374	2,397	2,816	2,696	2,834	3,366	42
Power-generating mach. & equip.	2,462	2,324	2,373	2,408	2,690	3,101	26
Prof., scientific & controlling instruments, etc.	2,009	1,935	2,111	2,152	2,266	2,504	25
Oilseeds & oleaginous fruit	3,888	3,081	2,764	1,824	2,111	2,153	-45
Mach. specialized for particular ind.	2,141	1,745	1,837	1,868	1,838	2,032	- 5
Misc. manufactured articles	1,411	1,324	1,304	1,244	1,489	1,869	32
Organic chemicals	1,358	1,141	1,246	1,406	1,334	1,752	29
Gen. industrial mach. & equip.	1,749	1,515	1,532	1,478	1,538	1,701	- 3
TOTAL	24,871	24,130	25,503	25,036	27,290	31,953	

Note: Totals may not add due to rounding.

*EC-12. Sectors are two-digit SITC categories, ranked by 1987 exports.

Source: Official statistics of the U.S. Department of Commerce.

APPENDIX B.   U.S. MERCHANDISE EXPORTS TO EC, 1960-87*
(Mill. $)

	1960	1965	1970	1975	1980	1985	1987
U.S. merchandise exports to EC	3,974	5,252	8,423	22,862	53,678	45,775	60,575
Total U.S. merchandise exports	19,650	26,461	43,197	108,856	225,566	218,815	252,853
% of total	20%	20%	19%	21%	24%	21%	24%

*EC-6 until 1973; EC-9 until 1981; EC-10 until 1986; EC-12 1986 and after.

Sources: *Statistical Abstract*, 1969; *Highlights of U.S. Export and Import Merchandise Trade* (U.S. Department of Commerce, Bureau of the Census), various issues; *Foreign Trade Highlights*, various issues; and *Economic Report of the President*, 1987.

APPENDIX C.   U.S. SERVICE EXPORTS TO EC, 1966-87*
(Mill. $)

	1966	1970	1975	1980	1985	1987
U.S. service exports to EC	946	1,029	4,504	9,168	11,213	17,478
Total U.S. service exports	6,885	8,052	19,289	36,876	47,066	59,968
% of total	14%	13%	23%	25%	24%	29%

*EC-6 until 1973; EC-9 until 1981; EC-10 until 1986; EC-12 1986 and after.

Source: *Survey of Current Business*, various issues.

APPENDIX D.   U.S. DIRECT INVESTMENT IN EC, 1960-87*
(Mill. $)

	1960	1965	1970	1975	1980	1985	1986	1987
U.S. direct invest. in EC	2,645	6,304	11,516	38,773	77,153	81,337	98,472	122,247
Total U.S. direct foreign invest.	31,865	49,474	75,480	124,050	215,375	229,748	259,562	308,793
% of total	8%	13%	15%	31%	36%	35%	38%	40%

*EC-6 until 1973; EC-9 until 1981; EC-10 until 1986; EC-12 1986 and after.

Sources: 1960–75, "Selected Data on U.S. Direct Investment Abroad, 1950–1976,"
          U.S. Department of Commerce, Bureau of Economic Affairs, February 1982;
          1980, *Survey of Current Business*, November 1984, p. 24;
          1985–86, *Survey of Current Business*, August 1987, p. 81; and
          1987, estimated Commerce Department figures.

Appendix E

Summary of the White Paper Proposals

The White Paper is divided into two parts. The first is a 50-page narrative, consisting of a description of the types of barriers to an integrated internal market, the problems they have created, the Commission's approach to overcoming these barriers, and, in some cases, specific proposals, including reference to those already before the Council. The second is the annex, listing about 300 measures for action necessary to "complete the internal market." This list identifies the subject of the proposal, documents previously made proposals, and indicates the year by which a proposal should be submitted by the Commission as well as the expected year for its adoption by the Council. The latest date for adoption is 1991, which was designed so as to leave at least one year for implementation of the measures by the member states.

The categorization of barriers listed in the White Paper is somewhat confusing. The first and third categories—physical and fiscal barriers—are readily understandable. However, the second one—technical barriers—is in effect a residual.

This appendix lists the categories of measures covered by the White Paper. It is neither exhaustive nor descriptive, but rather is intended to indicate the general subject matter under each category of barriers.

PART I. THE REMOVAL OF PHYSICAL BARRIERS

(1) Control of goods

(A) Miscellaneous: measures aimed at the abolition of import formalities and controls on goods at the border, including simplification of transit procedures, abolition of controls on truck quotas, duty-free admission of fuel contained in fuel tanks of commercial vehicles, Single Administrative Document, statistical harmonization, and elimination of national quotas.

(B) Veterinary and phytosanitary (plant health) controls: 71 measures (nearly one-fourth of the total) range across the plant and animal health field, from pesticide residue levels, food labeling and the role of the Community in health inspection to brucellosis in small ruminants, pedigree animals not covered in existing directives and the certification of reproductive materials in fruit plants.

(2) Control of individuals

(A) Monetary and fiscal exemptions for travelers, approximation of arms legislation, abolition of police controls, approximation of drugs legislation, coordination of rights of asylum and status of refugees, coordination of national visa policies, and rules on extradition.

PART II. THE REMOVAL OF TECHNICAL BARRIERS

(1) Free movement of goods

(A) New approach in technical harmonization and standards policy: information procedures on standards and technical rules, recognition of tests and certificates, and specific sector proposals (e.g., construction, machine safety, pressure vessels, and electromedical equipment).

(B) Sectoral proposals concerning approximation of laws: motor vehicles, tractors and agricultural machines, food, pharmaceuticals and high technology medicines, chemical products, construction and construction products, and miscellaneous items.

(2) Public procurement: improvement of existing directives, extension of directives to excluded sectors, services procurement, public works procurement, and implementation of directives.

(3) Free movement for labor and the professions: migrant workers, income tax harmonization, vocational training and qualifications, student mobility, apprentices, youth exchanges, advanced training on new technologies, recognition of pharmaceutical training, mutual recognition of higher education diplomas, and right of residence for nonemployed people.

(4) Common market for services

(A) Financial services

(i) Banks: accounts, mortgage credit, harmonization of "own funds" concept, large exposures, and coordination of credit institutions.

(ii) Insurance: nonlife, life, credit and automobile liability insurance, and insurance contracts.

(iii) Securities: collective investment undertakings, publication of information, prospectuses, and investment advisors.

(B) Transportation: air transportation fares, bilateral agreements and antitrust, road transportation quotas, bus services, inland waterway and ocean transportation, and nonresident carriers.

(C) New technologies and services: radio and television advertising, copyright of cable transmissions, information services, payment cards, and compatibility of system networks.

(5) Liberalization of capital movements: mortgage transactions, mutual funds, and securities operations.

(6) Creation of suitable conditions for industrial cooperation

(A) Company law: European Economic Interest Grouping, structure of public limited companies, cross-border mergers, separate accounts, liquidation of companies, takeover bids, relationship of undertakings in a group, and European company statutes.

(B) Intellectual and industrial property: approximation of trademark law, Community trademark, office site and fees, Community patent convention and appeal court, protection of biotechnology, computer programs, and microcircuits.

(C) Taxation: double taxation, parents and subsidiaries, mergers and divisions, and transactions in securities.

(7) Application of company law: transparency, state aids inventory and implications report.

PART III. THE REMOVAL OF FISCAL BARRIERS

(1) Value-added tax: standstill, small business, deductibles, refunds, temporary importation, abolition of derogations, rate structure, common rates, and clearing house system.

(2) Excise duties: standstill, harmonization on alcoholic beverages, manufactured tobacco, mineral oils, common rate bands, and bonded warehouse linkage.

Selected Bibliography

Albert, Michael and Ball, James. *Towards European Economic Recovery in the 1980s: Report to the European Parliament* New York: Praeger Special Studies, 1984.

Cecchini, Paolo. *The European Challenge 1992.* Aldershot, U.K.: Wildwood House, distributed in the United States by Gower Publishing Company, 1988.

Commission of the European Communities. "Completing the Internal Market," White Paper from the Commission to the European Council." COM(85) 310, June 14, 1985.

_____. "Third Report from the Commission to the Council and the European Parliament on the Implementation of the Commission's White Paper on Completing the Internal Market." Brussels: COM(88) 134, March 21, 1988.

EC Committee of the American Chamber of Commerce in Belgium. *Business Guide to EC Initiatives.* Brussels: Spring 1988.

The Economist. "Europe's Internal Market," survey (July 9, 1988).

Financial Times. "1992—Countdown to Reality" (February-March 1988).

Office for Official Publications of the European Communities. *Europe without Frontiers - Completion of the Internal Market* Luxembourg: European Documentation periodical 3/1988 (March 1988).

Padoa-Schioppa, Tommaso. *Efficiency, Stability and Equity: a Strategy for the Evolution of the Economic System of the European Community.* Oxford: Oxford University Press, 1988.

Pelkmans, Jacques. "An Enterprising Community." *SAIS Review* (January 1988).

_____. "A Grand Design by the Piece?," in *1992: One European Market?,* eds. Roland Bieber, *et al.* Florence: European University Institute, 1988.

Pelkmans, Jacques, and Winters, Alan. *Europe's Domestic Market,* Royal Institute of International Affairs Chatham House Papers No. 43. London: Routledge, 1988.

Philip, Alan Butt. *Implementing the European Internal Market: Problems and Prospects,* Royal Institute of International Affairs Discussion Paper No. 5. London: 1988.

Index

Academic degrees. *See* Professional qualifications

Agriculture, 7, 18, 22, 91. *See also* Plant and animal health

Albert-Ball report, 8, 65

American Chamber of Commerce in Belgium, EC Committee of the, 99, 100-101

Antidumping, 85, 89, 96, 97

Antitrust. *See* Competition policy

Asian countries. *See* Japan; Newly industrializing countries

Austria, 72

Automobiles, 83-85, 89, 102-104, 120

Banking: actions on and prospects for, 53-54, 58; description of barriers in, 25; and EFTA, 98; interest in insurance, 107; Italian, 37; reciprocity for, 88, 105; sectoral description of, 104-106; U.S. presence in, 78

Barriers, 1, 5, 20-27, 81-82

Beer (court decision). *See* European Court of Justice

Belgium, 23, 25, 30, 43, 109, 111

Border controls, 7, 8, 21-22, 38-40, 81, 104

Broadcasting, 25, 57, 123

Brussels, 13, 35, 40, 99, 100, 123, 126-127

Budget, Community, 14, 18, 29, 32-33, 67, 96

Capital movements, 5, 6, 24-25, 38, 51-53, 81, 104

Card payment systems, 54-55

Cassis de Dijon (court decision). *See* European Court of Justice

Cecchini report, 65-66, 73n, 87, 103, 114

CEN (European Standards Committee), 59-60, 91, 109

CENELEC (European Electrotechnical Standards Committee), 59-60, 91, 109

Central bank, European, 52, 70-71

CEPT (Conference of European Administrations of Posts and Telecommunications), 117

Certification. *See* Standards, technical

Civil aviation. *See* Transportation

Cockfield, Lord, 9, 36, 66

COCOM (Coordinating Committee on Multilateral Export Controls), 122-123

Commission, European: and border controls, 39; and capital movements, 51-53; and Cecchini report, 65-66; and competition policy, 18, 48-51; and copyright, 46; description of, 13, 14; and directives, 15-16, 36; and export controls, 122; and medical devices, 109; and monetary cooperation, 71; "1992" launch, 7, 32; and pharmaceuticals, 112-113; and public procurement, 61-63, 87; and regulations and standards, 90; relations with member states, 126; relations with other EC institutions, 16, 35, 126; and services, 53-57, 105; and small and medium sized enterprises, 69; and social policy, 47-48; and taxation, 42-44; and telecommunications, 114-116; U.S. relations with, 100, 126-127; and White Paper, 9-10, 29, 37-38

Common Agricultural Policy, 22

Common commercial policy, 5, 6

Common currency, 20, 70-71

National Planning Association

NPA is an independent, private, nonprofit, nonpolitical organization that carries on research and policy formulation in the public interest. NPA was founded during the Great Depression of the 1930s when conflicts among the major economic groups—business, labor, agriculture—threatened to paralyze national decisionmaking on the critical issues confronting American society. It was dedicated to the task of getting these diverse groups to work together to narrow areas of controversy and broaden areas of agreement and to provide on specific problems concrete programs for action planned in the best traditions of a functioning democracy. Such democratic planning, NPA believes, involves the development of effective governmental and private policies and programs not only by official agencies but also through the independent initiative and cooperation of the main private sector groups concerned. And to preserve and strengthen American political and economic democracy, the necessary government actions have to be consistent with, and stimulate the support of, a dynamic private sector.

NPA brings together influential and knowledgeable leaders from business, labor, agriculture, and the applied and academic professions to serve on policy committees. These committees identify emerging problems confronting the nation at home and abroad and seek to develop and agree upon policies and programs for coping with them. The research and writing for these committees are provided by NPA's professional staff and, as required, by outside experts.

In addition, NPA's professional staff undertakes research designed to provide data and ideas for policymakers and planners in government and the private sector. These activities include research on national goals and priorities, productivity and economic growth, welfare and dependency problems, employment and manpower needs, and technological change; analyses and forecasts of changing international realities and their implications for U.S. policies; and analyses of important new economic, social and political realities confronting American society. In developing its staff capabilities, NPA has increasingly emphasized two related qualifications. First is the interdisciplinary knowledge required to understand the complex nature of many real-life problems. Second is the ability to bridge the gap between theoretical or highly technical research and the practical needs of policymakers and planners in government and the private sector.

All NPA reports are authorized for publication in accordance with procedures laid down by the Board of Trustees. Such action does not imply agreement by NPA board or committee members with all that is contained therein unless such endorsement is specifically stated.